# Breaking the Assignment of
# Spiritual Assassins

# Breaking the Assignment of Spiritual Assassins

*Michael Pitts*

**M.A.P.S. Institute, Inc.**
Toledo, Ohio

Unless otherwise indicated, all scriptural quotations are from the *King James Version* of the Bible.

*Breaking the Assignment of Spiritual Assassins*
Published by:
M.A.P.S. Institute, Inc.
www.cornerstonechurch.us
ISBN 0-9726718-1-1


*Third Printing, October 2004*

Printed in the United States of America.

# Contents

# Foreword

This book, directed toward defying and defeating spiritual assassins, can be a real blessing to its readers.

When I was a missionary in the Philippines, I found the nation under much spiritual oppression. There was obviously a spirit which had been assigned to hinder revival in the country. I came face-to-face with that hindering spirit when I encountered a girl who was bitten by devils. Her deliverance triggered a revival in that nation. So I can testify I have personally seen the victory which can be had over such assassins.

The total victory of the believer comes from the resurrected Lord and Savior who declared that all power in heaven and earth had been delivered unto Him. He further declared that the very keys of death and hell were in His resurrected hands.

This assures every disciple of the Lord Jesus Christ that freedom, that every source of demonic oppression can be removed by a trust in Christ.

The author goes right to his point and shows you the way to total victory.

May the Lord richly bless you.

*Lester Sumrall*

# Breaking the Assignment of Spiritual Assassins

# Introduction

Man lives in two worlds simultaneously: one of matter and one of spirit.

The effects of the world of the spirit upon the human condition are far reaching. In this book, we will touch on only a few; we will only scratch the surface. Yet in doing so, it is my prayer that new understanding and insight will flood your heart and mind, causing you to reach new levels of freedom!

Michael S. Pitts

# Chapter 1

# The Reality of the Spirit Realm

It *is* possible for people to have spirits that have been assigned to them by the devil.

Often as a pastor I have seen evidence of this in people whose lives rapidly started to disintegrate. First one trouble hit them and then another, until it pulled them down.

Suddenly, people who we used to see on a regular basis are out of church for six or seven weeks. Then, before long, they are no longer serving God; they are no longer in the flow of God. They have been assassinated by the devil!

This truth was revealed to me as I was flying home from Fort Worth, and I began to intercede for my congregation individually and corporately.

## Assigned Spirits

As I prayed, the Lord dropped a phrase in my heart. I had never heard it before, nor had I ever heard anyone teach on it. It was a revelation to me.

The Lord said, "Many people in regions, churches, and families have spirits that have been assigned to them by the devil. The job of these spirits is to wait for these people to arrive at a place in life where they are ready to do something great — and then 'assassinate' them and take them out of commission." For an example from the natural world, consider this: No one ever wanted to assassinate Jimmy Carter when he was a peanut farmer.

But when he became President of the United States, he had to surround himself with bodyguards — he had to make sure he was protected — because when you get to be the President or in a similar high office, there may be those who wish to harm you!

## Spirits Assigned to Families

I will show you from scripture that often a spirit has been assigned to individuals or families, and it will be the main spirit they will battle all the days of their lives. The spirit that is upon the father or the mother may be transmitted down to their offspring. Frequently, this spirit begins its attack when a person is very young. You must learn how to break family spirits.

At times the spirit will remain dormant, but when a person gets ready to make a big move for God, it will rise up to assassinate him, and he will fall back into a low position once again.

*This cycle of slight victories followed by defeats will be repeated throughout the person's life.* He will find himself fighting the same problem over and over again, perhaps seeking counseling or other help, not realizing that counseling can only help *after* the spirit is removed.

I am not against counseling, but you can't "counsel" a demon out of someone! However, when you break the demonic force over someone's life, counseling will then help the person.

A couple can get marriage counseling, but unless they recognize that a spirit has been assigned to their family to destroy them, all the counseling in the world won't solve their relational problems. As a matter of fact, many times the couple will just use the counseling to blame each other for their marital situation.

Instead, they should get into agreement and realize that *a family spirit* has been assigned to them to utterly destroy their family. After they have put that spirit to flight, counseling may help them work things out.

## A Spirit of Poverty

If a spirit has been assigned to you to destroy your finances, you can go to every "get rich" seminar around, you can get financial advice from brilliant bankers, and you can even have a lot of money — but your financial problems will continue. Did you know you can have a lot of money and still be bound by *a spirit of poverty?*

*Poverty doesn't have to do with economics; it is a spiritual problem!* Although we have an enormous amount of money in this nation, we also have people devastated by the spirit of poverty. Although we're the richest nation on the planet, there are still people who go hungry.

You can have a lot of money and still be in financial trouble. Ask Donald Trump about it. Just because you have a lot of money does not mean that poverty has not attached itself to you.

However, even if you have been raised in poverty, you don't have to remain in poverty all your life. It doesn't matter if *all* your relatives were in poverty; *you can break the curse of poverty!*

You should not allow what limited your forefathers spiritually to destroy you. Somewhere down that blood line, someone has to rise up, get under the blessing, and break the curse. *Do it in Jesus' Name!*

## Why Great People Fall

As I began to study people's lives, one thing surprised and puzzled me, and I asked, "Lord, why do great people fall? Whether they're political, religious, civic, business, or family leaders, suddenly, at moments of great potential, their faults come to public attention. How did they ever get to a position of such prominence with lives so out of order?"

Then the Lord revealed to me that it's because the spirit assigned to them had actually pulled back for a season to allow them to gain notoriety — *because the more prominent you are when you fall, the more people you take down with you.*

Some people will tell me this message has nothing to do with Christians. Obviously, they haven't talked to some of the Christians I've talked to!

I want to point out that just because you are a Christian doesn't mean the devil has stopped fighting you.

## Guardian Angels vs. Assigned Spirits

I believe that when you're born, God assigns you a guardian angel. I believe that when you're expecting a child, you should seek God for the name and the destiny of that child. My wife, Kathi, and I began to read the Bible over our children when they were still in her womb, praying over them and so forth.

I also believe that when a child is born, the devil may send a spirit after him that, if not detected and defeated, the child will wrestle against most of the days of his life.

To see this in scripture, let's look at the sixth chapter of Matthew, where Jesus was teaching His disciples to pray. He said:

> **After this manner therefore pray ye: Our Father which art in heaven, Hallowed be thy name.**
> **Thy kingdom come. Thy will be done in earth as it is in heaven.**
> **Give us this day our daily bread.**
> **And forgive us our debts, as we forgive our debtors. And lead us not into temptation, *but deliver us from evil*....**
> **Matthew 6:9-13**

The Weymouth translation says, "Deliver us from the evil one."

Christians need to be delivered from the plan of the evil one! Technically, we *were* delivered by Jesus' sacrifice on Calvary, but the devil still assaults us. Therefore, we need to pray when we wake up, "Lord, this day deliver me from the plan of the evil one."

We don't pray in fear, but in faith. Faith, however, demands we walk in the knowledge of our battles; not in ignorance and denial of them.

## The Evil One

As we lay a scriptural foundation here, starting with the basics, the first principle to remember is: There is an evil one — just in case someone told you there's not. In fact, the Bible states in First Peter 5:8:

> **Be sober, be vigilant; because your adversary the devil, as a roaring lion, walketh about, seeking whom he may devour.**

And there is not only *an evil one;* there is also *an evil day,* as we see in the following passage from Ephesians 6.

> **Finally, my brethren, be strong in the Lord, and in the power of his might.**
> **Put on the whole armour of God, that ye may be able to stand against the wiles of the devil.**
> **For we wrestle not against flesh and blood, but against principalities, against powers, against the rulers of the darkness of this world, against spiritual wickedness in high** [or heavenly] **places.**
> **Wherefore take unto you the whole armour of God, that ye may be able to withstand** *in the evil day....*
> **Ephesians 6:10–13**

We discover that we are in a battle — a wrestling match — not against flesh and blood, but against demonic principalities, powers, rulers, and wickedness; and we must put on the whole armor of God.

## The Evil Day

These scriptures seem to infer that if we do not have on the whole armor of God, and *the evil one* comes and brings *an*

7

*evil day,* we may not be able to stand.

When you see Christians who have fallen by the way-side, it could be because: (1) they weren't wearing the whole armor of God; (2) they didn't recognize the evil one; and (3) they didn't even know they were in an evil day. Therefore, they were not able to stand.

Paul, writing to Timothy, tells us *when* the evil day is.

**Now the Spirit speaketh expressly, that in the latter times some shall depart from the faith, giving heed to seducing spirits, and doctrines of devils.**

**1 Timothy 4:1**

Paul said, "The evil day is the last days. In the last days there will be seducing spirits and doctrines of devils." Paul speaks further of the last days in Second Timothy.

**This know also, that in the last days perilous times shall come....**

**2 Timothy 3:1**

The point is: There is an evil one. There is an evil day. The evil days are the last days — and we are living in those last days!

But the good news is this: There is also a *Greater One* who will bring us a *greater day* and lead us into *a new day!*

# Chapter 2

# Breaking the Assignments of Spiritual Assassins

This revelation about breaking the assignments of spiritual assassins is powerful when you see and understand it. It has answered many questions that I have had as a result of witnessing the operation of spirit beings in the affairs of people through what the Bible calls the gift of "discerning of spirits."

Don't get far out with this teaching, however. Balance it with other truth in the Word of God. Many people say they are "discerning spirits" when they are really just suspicious of people; and, particularly, everyone who ever treated them badly. They think they are discerning demon activity, but they aren't. Some people just don't like you, and others have nasty dispositions, but it doesn't mean they're demon possessed!

Yet the truth still exists that *many people do what they do because they are motivated and dominated by unseen forces that are controlling their lives.* Inside, they don't want to act the way they do, but they find themselves powerless against the forces that are at work in their lives.

## Molestation: The Spiritual Root

Sometimes strolling in the mall or praying with people in churches I see, through the discerning of spirits, children with *a spirit of molestation* upon them.

9

This means that if you put that child in a room with 50 other children and then you add an adult who has a spirit to molest children, he will select that child out of all the rest!

That's why some children are molested more than once in their lifetime. And the devil is so cruel, he convinces them that because it has happened to them more than once, they've done something to attract the molester.

The children don't know it was an assigned spirit that drew upon the evil within that adult, and those two spirits from the devil orchestrated the events, managing to put that child and that adult together, creating a sinister scenario of prey and predator.

Parents, realize we are living in the last days; in perilous times. There is an evil one. Learn how to cover your children with prayer. Teach them the Word of God and how to discern spirits.

Children have better discernment than adults do, because we adults learn how to lie to each other and suppress our discernment. But children have good discernment, and you need to teach them how to act appropriately when they use it.

You also need to cover them in the Word of God and prayer, and you need to be spiritually astute enough to discern if some spirit has been assigned to your child.

Why is it that I can spot the spirit of molestation upon children whose parents are blind to it?

Did you know unsaved people operate in discernment, and they don't even know what it is? For example, when some sinners go to a nightclub, they unknowingly operate in discernment.

This man knows he's only going to be at this club for two hours, and he's planning to take some woman to bed tonight. He doesn't have time to go through the crowd and talk to a lot of women who will turn him down, so he stands and scans the room. He's got to find someone who will be willing to go along with him. He is discerning and relating to unclean spirits, and he doesn't even know it. The spirit of lust is upon him, drawing him to a willing accomplice.

## The Key to Abusive Relationships

Why is it that women who have been involved in one abusive relationship tend to gravitate in subsequent relationships toward the same kind of man who treats them badly? You couldn't pick that many losers out of a hat if you tried, so how do you find all of them?

It's because there's a spirit that has been assigned to you to destroy your life, and there's a spirit inside that man that always wants to mistreat you. And those two spirits are orchestrating the events of your life, because their job is to assassinate you and destroy you!

But you can break the devil's power through the Word of God and go free in Jesus' Name!

## Territorial Spirits

We have seen that there are spirits that are assigned to individuals and families — but there are also spirits that are assigned to certain regions of the earth. They are called *territorial spirits.* This is the second principle you need to understand about demon spirits.

You cannot win an individual, a family, or a city until you break the assignment of the devil that is against them. In First Corinthians 15:32, Paul referred to fighting "the beasts at Ephesus." He knew there were territorial spirits assigned over that region.

You will remember from the Book of Daniel that Daniel's prayers were hindered for 21 days in the heavenly realm until the angel Michael came and engaged the hindering spirits in spiritual warfare. Daniel 10:13 speaks of "the prince of the kingdom of Persia" and "the kings of Persia."

Spirits are assigned to regions in our own country, too. Inner cities have spirits that are assigned to them, and suburbs have spirits that are assigned to them.

Many times when you see a high concentration of the manifestations of the domination of darkness and destruction in a geographic area, a territorial spirit is at work. Interestingly enough, these spirits have an unusual ability to keep their victims within the borders of their unseen prison.

People under the oppressive force of poverty may move several times a year, yet never leave a particular area of town. I have seen some move many times within the same 20-block radius. Therefore, although they are always on the move, they never really go anywhere!

I have seen three and four generations of family members grow up in little country towns with substandard schooling, astronomical teen pregnancy and suicide rates, an out-of-control alcohol problem, and a history of family break-ups due to adultery. Yet they remain — almost oblivious to the spiritual climate they are in — *until it hits home!*

There is a reason why prostitutes walk certain streets; why drugs are easily accessible in *certain* neighborhoods. There is a reason why things like suicide, pregnancy, and rape will hit a school and spread in almost epidemic proportions.

There is a reason why perverts meet in certain *parks* and why occult activity is prevalent in one area while vandalism is dominant in another. The answer to all of this is *territorial spirits.*

## Spirits and Drugs

The Greek word for "drugs" is *pharmakia*, which is also translated as "sorcery." Drugs produce altered states of consciousness in human beings. Drugs may be used by unclean spirits as instruments of bondage — and *these addictions can be broken, because they have spiritual roots.*

When I was in a mostly Hispanic area of East Los Angeles one year, I learned that the main drug used there is *heroin.* It has been handed down from generation to generation in some families.

Often a spirit of insanity is attached to heroin. The unholy alliance of religious superstitions, palm reading, candle burning, contact with the dead, and statue worship passed from generation to generation create a culture conducive to the spirits of witchcraft, mind control, and insanity.

Crack, which is primarily distributed in the inner cities of America, has a *spirit of violence* attached to it. Wherever there is a high concentration of the sale of crack, there is also a high concentration of violence.

Crack is a violence-producing drug that opens people up to a spirit of rage and violence, and causes them to kill people, whether strangers during minor robberies, members of rival gangs, or family members who are perceived as hindrances to the furthering of the addiction.

If you know someone who is addicted to crack, you must protect yourself from that spirit of violence, for if you confront the person at the wrong time in the wrong environment, the spirit of rage and violence will rise up in him, and he will try to attack you.

Alcoholism opens people up for a different spirit than crack or heroin. Every spirit has its own characteristics and functions in different ways. People who are bound by depressants have a totally different spirit. Instead of attacking you, they may withdraw totally, because depressants have a depressing spirit attached to them that will bring the person to a point of suicide.

Alcohol is just one of many depressants which may cause its victim to flee responsibility, withdraw from family and friends, and eventually produce a defeated spirit within the person who is bound.

Males and females have specific spirits assigned to them, and some spirits are more prevalent in one sex than the other. For example, *the spirits of perversion or pornography* are more specifically assigned to men than to women. (This doesn't mean women are not operating in these things, but they attach themselves more frequently to men.)

*The spirits of rejection* and *manipulation* that break up so many families are assigned more frequently to women than they are to men.

We see all these tragedies happening in our society, and they are caused by assigned spirits.

## Spirits Assigned to Individuals

Individuals can have spirits that have been assigned to them.

King Saul had a spirit that was assigned to him to destroy him, and he eventually killed himself. First Samuel 16:14 says, "The Spirit of the Lord departed from Saul, and an evil spirit from the Lord troubled Saul."

In Second Corinthians 12:7, Paul wrote, "And lest I should be exalted above measure through the abundance of the revelations, there was given to me a thorn in the flesh, the messenger of Satan [a spirit] to buffet me...." Paul knew that a spirit was assigned to him. He fought this spirit all the days of his life.

Even Jesus had a spirit assigned to Him! But Jesus was so powerful, only the top demon — Satan himself — would dare to approach Him. Satan was assigned to Jesus. His assignment while Jesus was on the earth was to assassinate Him!

We know from the fourth chapter of Luke that Satan first tried to entice Jesus to kill himself by jumping off the pinnacle of the Temple. When he couldn't tempt Jesus to commit suicide, he tried to incite mobs against Jesus, and eventually he did get the people to kill Jesus.

Always remember, *before your ascension comes your assassination attempt.* The devil knows when you're getting ready to make a step up spiritually, so he *naturally* wants to take you out. Therefore, like Jesus, you have to fight the power of the devil.

**And Jesus being full of the Holy Ghost returned from Jordan, and was led by the Spirit into the wilderness,**

**Being forty days tempted of the devil....**

**And when the devil had ended all the temptation, he departed from him [Jesus]** *for a season.*

**Luke 4:1,2,13**

14

*For a season!* This is one of the ways the devil keeps a lifelong hold on people. We sometimes feel that if we're not in the middle of a crisis, everything must be all right. Understand that spirits which are assigned to destroy people will come *for a season.*

They will grab a person's desires, mind, family, and/or finances, and cause every kind of havoc you can think of. Then, just before they are detected, they will loosen their hold, and the person will experience a season of renewed freedom. They will get that bill paid, will experience a season where they don't argue with their spouse, or will quit drinking for a season.

In fact, some alcoholics quit drinking for six months at a time, and everyone thinks they're fine. But, all of a sudden, the desire to drink comes back on them again.

Assigned spirits cause these *cycles of defeat,* and that's how a person lives for 10, 20, 40, or 50 years with the same spiritual force battling for his life. It comes for a season, goes for a season, returns for a season, and leaves for a season. Part of its strategy is to remain undetected.

If it stays long enough, eventually you're going to say, "There's a demon causing this." But as long as you say, "It's my wife causing this," the demon is safe.

## Targeted for Assassination

I've seen what happens to Christian individuals or families who become the target of spiritual assassination. A crisis suddenly happens in their lives — a death in the family, a financial setback, or some other disaster. The crisis takes them out of the picture. It "throws them for a loop," as we say.

When they try to get motivated to return to church, their car breaks down and they can't get there. Then, without warning, they lose their job, or their daughter is pregnant, and before we realize it, they are out of church for six weeks. They want to return, but they find themselves unable to do so.

Nothing is going to change in such a situation until you recognize that you have been targeted for assassination. Rather than trying to solve your problems in the natural realm, you as an individual, a couple, or a family must come together and realize that you have been targeted for assassination. Then you need to push that evil power out of your life! *Greater is He that is in you than he that is in the world!*

Don't think it's a small thing when circumstances pull you out of the house of God and so consume your thoughts, energy, and resources that you begin to lose your desire for the things of God. It could be the first step on the road to your assassination! Many are assassinated because they didn't know they were targeted.

## How the Devil Infiltrates

To make a natural analogy, if someone is plotting to assassinate a public figure, the job of the assassin is to remain undetected. If everyone knows he is an assassin, he can't carry out his assignment. He has to hide. He has to be a sniper. He has to fit in and infiltrate without being spotted.

Likewise, the devil comes in many ways and disguises to infiltrate your life, staying long enough to cause you problems and maintain his hold, but disappearing behind the scenes before he's spotted. I'm going to teach you how to spot him.

One of the ways the devil infiltrates your life is by working on your *desires*. Many people don't understand when something is caused by a demon power, because they believe it's their own inner desire.

If you have a desire for things that are wrong, that desire didn't originate with you. How do you get a desire for substances like drugs or alcohol that destroy the body? That is an unclean desire, and it is from the devil.

I am going to teach you things that counseling can never accomplish. Counseling can teach you self-discipline so you won't do a thing, but many people still have the inner desire to do it.

The Bible speaks about "the inward parts," "the reins," or even "the belly," which refer to the place of desire and control. Jesus said, "He that believeth on me, as the scripture said, Out of his *belly* shall flow rivers of living water" (John 7:38). He was referring to your inner man.

David said in Psalm 139:13, "For thou [God] hast possessed my *reins*..." (*King James Version*); "For Thou didst form my *inward parts*..." (*American Standard Version*).

If a devil gets hold of you in your inner man, he will pull you by your "reins," or your inward desires. People who are bound, whether by pornography, drug addiction, bitterness, or something else, are bound in their inward desires. Many times they may even feel a tightness or a weight which seems located in their belly. In their head, they know their actions are wrong. In their head, they don't want to do it — but something on the inside of them begins to pull on them.

That is why men who are violent and beat their wives and children often return to them afterwards, repent, and say they're sorry. But the problem is inside them, not in their head. You can talk and talk to them, kiss them, and pat them all you want to, but the problem is who is holding the reins controlling the desires of the inner man.

Meanwhile, the devil goes undetected, because he convinces us that it's our desires that cause us to act the way we do. Actually, it is a spirit that has been assigned to control those desires.

When you get born again and the devil is put out, you get new desires. The Bible says, "As newborn babes, desire the sincere milk of the word" (1 Peter 2:2).

If you had an altar experience, but you don't want to go to church, and we've got to follow you around for six weeks and beg you to come back, you didn't get saved. You just said in your head, "I don't want to go to hell." Big deal! The devil doesn't want to go to hell, either, but he's going. There will be a lot of people in hell who don't want to be there.

There is a difference between a head decision and a heart that becomes submitted to the lordship of Jesus Christ.

Submit yourself to God, resist the devil, and he *will* flee from you! *He will flee from you* (James 4:7)!

Christians sometimes get caught up in wrong desires. They watch wrong things, and when they do, it creates wrong desires. They also listen to wrong things.

Do you know people can get an unclean desire for gossip? They're not happy unless someone says, "Did you hear about So-and-so?" Their heart starts beating faster when they hear this. They perk up. They get excited about it, but it's an unclean desire — a spirit.

Free yourself today from anything that seeks to produce unclean desires, and let your heart be toward God.

# Chapter 3

# Manifestations of Spiritual Assassins

One of the most fascinating revelations about demons is that they often remain undetected because they do not always reveal themselves in the same way.

In the first place, they try to keep themselves hidden. Also, to throw you off track, they reveal or manifest themselves in ways you're not expecting. It is extremely important for you to understand this.

As we have seen, there are different classifications of spirits — principalities, powers, and so forth — and different levels of authority with spirits. Spirits can be linked together. Often they have a "general," to use a military analogy, over them whose authority is divided into different classifications.

This means that *many spirits that appear to us in the natural to be complete opposites are actually the same spirit at work.* They have simply manifested themselves in a different way so we won't put two and two together and cast them out!

## Adultery and Poverty

For example, *the spirit of adultery and the spirit of poverty are governed by the same spirit!* You can see how absurd that sounds to the natural mind, but let's look at it according to biblical principles.

Whoever you lay with gets your money. We, as God's people, need to know this. The massage parlors know it. The prostitutes know it. Men who have children by five and six women know it. *Whoever you lay with gets your money.* That's why poverty comes upon those who are promiscuous and allow adultery. A lot is being said today (as it should be) about helping our black communities to be economically empowered. We are all concerned with the rising number of our teens of every race who are sexually active. The point is that our answers are not economic; they are spiritual.

In our black communities, the enemy has taken advantage of the crimes and wounds of slavery to further perpetuate a legacy of broken families. When this is not dealt with by God's Word and Spirit, it produces an openness and tolerance for adultery, which then brings the fruit of poverty. Thus, Satan's goal of bondage is achieved, for although a person can be legally free economically, he can still remain a slave to the system.

I am not trying to insinuate that black people are the only ones fooling around; that would be foolish. I am using a strong example to make a strong point. Whatever your race, you can break generational curses!

It doesn't matter if it's addictions, poverty, divorces, traumas, or destruction — through God's power, you and your seed can be blessed. Say it now: *"I am blessed."* Believe it, live like it, and go free in Jesus' Name!

## Rape and Murder

*Rape and murder are twin spirits.* Did you know that? Many times in the Bible where a man raped a woman, that man died a terrible death. If God didn't kill him, He often sent someone to do it. A famous missionary-evangelist once told me, "Anyone who will lust after your flesh will kill it." And you find this is true throughout the Bible. Rape and murder are twin spirits.

Many times we have seen where an important official has an affair, and afterwards the woman blackmailed him or

20

exposed him and assassinated his character. And sometimes the man got tired of the woman he had an affair with, and he murdered her or had her murdered. He was lusting after her one day, and he killed her the next. Do you see how these things are tied together?

Some of you have experienced such things in your life and in your family's lives. A well-known television evangelist had a spirit that was assigned to him to destroy him. When he committed adultery, he lost everything he had. You can't sin and be blessed.

## Alcoholic and Workaholic

An alcoholic father who never earned a dime in his life can produce a son who becomes a millionaire because he's a workaholic. *An alcoholic and a workaholic are the same spirit;* they just manifest themselves in different ways!

So you can have an alcoholic dad living in a shack, doing nothing, and his son can end up owning a million-dollar business. People will say to the son, "You're *nothing* like your dad," when, in fact, he has the same spirit his dad had! That's how these spirits go undetected.

The demon will disguise itself. It knows if all the members of a family are alcoholics, sooner or later someone in the family is going to be smart enough to catch on; however, most of these spirits have been in families for generations, and no one has uncovered them yet. So the spirit will make one an alcoholic, one a workaholic, one a shopaholic, one a foodaholic, and so forth.

## When Demons Panic

Whenever you see an out-of-balance reaction to a comment or an environment, it is possible that a demon is getting close to being exposed. Otherwise, it keeps mutating and using a different way of operating in your family so no one ever finds out that the same spirit is behind everyone's problems.

When you get a direct hit, people overreact. I preach quite straight, and when some people hear me, they overreact. They want to get up and run out, or lash out.

Do you know what that is called? It's called "your demon knows if it stays much longer, I'm going to expose it so clearly that even your crazy self is going to know it."

Of course I am not saying that everyone who doesn't enjoy my preaching has a demon. But some people become angry and hostile anytime you bring up the name of our church in conversation. Such an overreaction is designed to protect that demon. You see, to sit and submit to the Word of God spells expulsion for that demon. That demon will be cast out and off your life, and you will be free. So the demon encourages you to overreact.

Suppose you tell a girl, "You're *just* like your mother," thinking you're giving her a compliment. Instead, she explodes, "What? What? I'm *nothing* like her!"

That's called an overreaction. And do you know what it means? It means it's very possible that she is battling the same spirit that her mother battled. She doesn't want to admit it, and the devil doesn't want you to find out about it. It wants her to overreact and act like she's nothing like her mother.

And that's why you get such a reaction out of your husband or wife when you look at them and say, "You act just like your daddy." It could be he had the same spirit.

## Transference of Spirits

*Spirits are passed down or assigned through families.* The spirits upon the father or the mother will be transferred to their children and other descendants unless they are stopped.

You have the power to break family spirits! You can't allow what killed your forefathers spiritually to destroy you as well. Somewhere down that blood line, someone has to rise up under the anointing of the Holy Spirit and break the curse in Jesus' Name!

So if you look through your family tree and find that every male has been an alcoholic, or every marriage has ended in divorce, please have compassion on your future spouse, and deal with that spirit before you get married. You must break it; otherwise, that spirit will manifest itself in your family.

Every family has certain weaknesses. Every family and every person has to battle something. If you don't break that thing, your children will have to break it.

Many of us are battling things our parents didn't have the understanding or the revelation to break. It wasn't that they were evil or were against you. Perhaps they didn't have the light you are now receiving.

When understanding and revelation come, they bring the power to break the assignment. Then, when your children are born, they are free. They have a level playing field; they don't have to start out in a deficit.

Read the Word of God over your children before they're born. Confess over them. Pray over them. Ask God what their destiny in life is, and then name them accordingly. In the Bible, a person's name was tied to his destiny. Don't name your child after an ungodly relative who lived a life of bondage and destruction.

## The Boy Who Changed His Name

I once prayed for a young teenager in our church whose name was "Plaz." He was involved in the Youth Department, but he always acted as if he felt he didn't belong. He wore a large hearing aid because he was born nearly deaf in one ear.

He came forward for prayer in one of our healing services. I prayed for him briefly and continued down the line praying for others. The next thing I knew, people were telling me, *"Plaz can hear!"*

That night as we returned to our Bible class, I walked up behind him. I noticed he wasn't wearing a hearing aid. Knowing that his hearing had been limited with it and next to nothing without it, I put him to the test. Standing a good distance behind him, I said softly, "How ya doing tonight, Plaz?" Without hesitation, he turned and said, "Great! I'm healed, Pastor!"

In the following weeks, I began to notice that Plaz was becoming more popular than he had ever been before. All this attention was bringing him out of his shell. He gave his testimony to the teen group and his friends at school. He even spoke to our Easter Sunday crowd that year.

Finally, with all the changes that were occurring in Plaz's life, he felt he needed one more. He changed his legal name from "Plaz" to Andrew Jackson! *Now, that's a name!*

## I Will Return Into My House

We find a description of family spirits in Matthew 12:

> **When the unclean spirit is gone out of a man, he walketh through dry places, seeking rest, and findeth none.**
> **Then he saith, I will return into my house from whence I came out; and when he is come, he findeth it empty, swept, and garnished.**
> **Then goeth he, and taketh with himself seven other spirits more wicked than himself, and they enter in and dwell there and the last state of that man is worse than the first.**
> **Matthew 12:43–45**

Notice the phrase "my house from whence I came out" in verse 44. The word "house" can also mean "household." For example, the Bible says that God put a hedge around Job and all of his "house."

If a man has a spirit that dominates his life, and the man dies through a tragedy like alcoholism or drug addiction, in a violent murder or something of that nature, or even commits suicide, that spirit has to leave him and go somewhere else when he dies. I'm not referring to casting a spirit out of a living person. You see, sometimes people die with spirits, and sometimes spirits even cause people to die before they have lived a full life.

After the man dies, the spirit comes out of him and says, "I've got to find a new home. Where should I go?" It decides, "I'll go back to the same household." It is already well acquainted with the weaknesses in the family.

For many generations, even Christians didn't have adequate teaching on this subject, so they were not successful in preventing a family spirit from getting into their families; and often when one of the family members died, the spirit returned to the same household.

It is possible that you are battling the same spirit your parents, grandparents, and aunts and uncles battled throughout their lifetimes. If so, it is the spirit that has been assigned to your bloodline to destroy your family members!

## Ways Spirits Enter

Have you noticed that sometimes after one teenager commits suicide, many other students in the same school will also commit suicide? Educators become alarmed, because once it hits, it's like an epidemic.

You can bring in clergy to counsel with the students, and that's a good thing; but the truth is, somehow, some way, that spirit has found a spiritual door open into the school. Until that door is shut and the devil is cast out of the school, many other children may commit suicide.

Rather than just counseling with the survivors, the educators should bring in a man of God who will cast the spirit out in the Name of Jesus, and let the children go free.

*Children can bring spirits in with them.* Not long ago, I talked on the telephone to a woman who claimed, "Spirits are in my house."

I replied, "They are? How do you know?"

She said, "When I wake up, the furniture has been moved in different positions. Things are broken. I hear things all night long."

"Are you alone in your house?"

"Yes."

I said, "Yes, that's a spirit." (Some people think their

25

house has spirits when it's just the trees outside rubbing up against the house.)

## The Open Door

So I told her, "Well, somehow a door was left open." I was not referring to a garage door; I was referring to a spiritual door — a way of access for the devil. "Somehow you opened the door for that to happen."

"No, no, no, no!" she protested.

Then the Lord began to give me a word of knowledge. Don't lie to someone who is under the anointing. The Lord said the spirit got in through this woman's children. When I said, "The devil got into your house through your children," she retorted, "I don't have any children in my house."

I said, "That's what the Lord told me."

She finally admitted, "Well, I *did* have children in my house."

"Now we're getting somewhere. Why did they leave?"

"Well, I was gone a lot of the time, and they got older, and they needed to move out."

"How old were they when they left?"

"One was 20 and one was 22."

I was still operating in the Spirit, and I said, "Did you ever leave them alone over the weekend, and when you came home, you found they'd had parties in your house?"

"Oh, yes, on several occasions."

I said, "Now we see where the door went open. You don't know who was at those parties, do you?"

She got very defensive, as if I was trying to accuse her children of being astrologers or satanists, but I didn't know whether they were or not.

I said, "Their friends might have been involved in something evil. You don't know *who* they brought into your house, or *what* they brought in with them."

She said, "Well, the priest came out and gave me some holy water and things like that."

I said, "You've still got a demon, haven't you?"

"Yes."

Demons aren't afraid of water. When Jesus cast devils out of a herd of pigs, where did they go? Straight into the water!

I told her, *"You can get that spirit out of your house. It doesn't have any right to be there."*

## Haunted Houses

There are people who will move out of a house they think is "haunted." It is true that if a murderer lived in a house and people were killed there, an evil spirit can be in that house. But I would never move out for a demon.

As a matter of fact, we ought to look for houses people say are haunted, because they are cheap. No one wants to live in them. When the realtor tells you, "This house is haunted," you can say, "Take another $10,000 off the price."

After you buy the house, on the day you move in, shut the door and say, "In the Name of Jesus, you foul spirit, you're not going to have this house! I cast you out in the Name of Jesus!"

Tell it to go. Don't play patty-cake with it. Tell it, "This is going to be a house dedicated to God. As a matter of fact, I'm getting ready to turn on some praise music. I'm going to get my Bible out. I'm going to call a prayer meeting." Then invite every radical, tongue-talking friend you've got for a Holy Ghost meeting, and put the devil out in Jesus' Name!

You put the devil out! Don't let the devil put *you* out of a house! If you have prayed for God to give you a house and you got it, don't let the devil run you out of it. *He* has to go, in Jesus' Name.

## Spiritual Bodyguards

Presidents or other prominent figures can be in danger of assassination because of their stand on certain issues, or simply because of their position. Therefore, they are surrounded by bodyguards and intelligence agents whose job

27

is to watch *where they cannot see. In order to assassinate them, their enemies usually have to get them away from the people who protect them.*

The same principle holds true in the spiritual realm. Each of us has a blind spot, so God will join people to our lives to act as bodyguards or intelligence officers for us. While we look one way, they look another way, and they become protection for us.

When we get ready to make a move, out of the corner of their eye they may see danger ahead, and they warn us, "Wait a minute! Ever since you hooked up with So-and-so, you've been acting crazy. You dress funny now, too. You don't praise God anymore. We used to talk about the Word, but you don't talk about the Word anymore. I think I see an assassin with his sights on you!"

*When the devil gets ready to assassinate you, he will try to pull you away from the people God has sent into your life to protect you* — people who love you, people who are not judging you or trying to hold you back, people who are acting as your intelligence agents.

When you're asked, "Why don't you associate with them anymore?" the devil will give you *religious* excuses. You will pout, "They don't *encourage* me." You want to be encouraged when you're doing wrong. You may need to be *rebuked,* not encouraged. You want someone to pity you. "They *offended* me," you whine. It probably means they got too close to exposing your demon.

## Ignoring Warnings

Those who are targeted for assassination by the devil won't listen to anyone. You can't tell them anything. If you try to rebuke them, they will turn around and rebuke *you.* But the Bible says, "Obey them that have the rule over you, and submit yourselves: *for they watch for your souls...*" (Hebrews 13:17).

Perhaps the pastor comes to that person and says, "Listen, I can't put my finger on it, but something's not right with you. What's going on in your life?"

The person retaliates, "Who are you talking to? *I'm as saved as you are!"*

Assassination is surely heading his way.

John 10 says that the Good Shepherd sees the wolf coming. *The shepherd sees things the sheep do not see.* Sheep are so nearsighted, they do not see the wolf until their head is in its mouth. When they see its tonsils, they finally say, "Ah, I think the wolf is coming."

To protect his flock from the wolf, the Good Shepherd has a rod and a staff. The staff pulls the sheep close to the shepherd, and the rod beats the wolf off. I am not afraid to be a shepherd. I pull people in. I beat demons off them.

## Hiding in a New Flock

When a person is targeted for assassination, the devil will pull him away from the house of God and the people who know him. He will seek a new group of friends who don't know how demonized he really is. All of us have weaknesses, and people who are close to us know about them.

I've known people who go from group to group. They have no long-lasting relationships. If you don't have any long-lasting relationships, you need to check yourself, because the devil may be trying to assassinate you by cutting you off from the rest of the Body of Christ.

When these wanderers go to a new group, everything is fine for two or three weeks. Then they encounter some kind of problem or conflict and get upset, so they go to another group. People who want money all the time frequently do this. After they get all they can from one group, they go to another. When they get all they can from the second group, they go on to a third.

## The Demonic Realm Is Real

When a spirit is identified, it will either run away, or it will totally manifest. I'm not referring to spooky stuff, but people need to understand that the demonic realm is real. You shouldn't be afraid of it, yet you should have a healthy respect for it. And if you live a halfhearted life, leave demon-possessed people alone.

Sometimes it is a painful experience when demons are cast out of someone, because they don't want to leave. The Bible says that unclean spirits would "tear" people as they came out of them.

I was in a service once when we began to pray for a man who had been addicted to drugs for a long time. The power of God came on this man to deliver him, and he began to cry out. This is scriptural. Acts 8:7 says, "For unclean spirits, crying with loud voice, came out of many that were possessed with them...."

This man cried until he began to bleed from his mouth, because that spirit did not want to leave him. It began to tear him, but it had to come out in Jesus' Name.

## The Joy of Freedom

The devil is rough on people when he holds them under his power, but he has to loose them and let them go free in the Name of Jesus. Acts 8:8 says that when the unclean spirits came out of the people of the city of Samaria, *"there was great joy in that city."*

When you put the devil out, joy comes to your house. When you put the devil out, joy comes to your city. When you put the devil out, joy comes to the church.

People who are bound by the devil are bound up on the inside. They have a "weight" that sits on the inside of them. They are tormented day and night, because they know they have been targeted by the devil. Someone has to come in Jesus' Name to set the captives free and to warn those who may be on the edge of falling into the devil's snare.

## Perilous Times

The devil may tell you, "I am going to give you a business deal that's so good, you're going to make a lot of money." But there's a catch to it: You won't be able to come to church for the next six months. You think you're pursuing a blessing, but you're walking right into the devil's sights to be taken out!

You have to know what God is saying. Perilous times are here, and the Lord wants to set you free. I am going to give you a natural illustration. It is plain, and I pray that no one misunderstands me.

Many ministers have been targeted for assassination, and spirits have also been assigned to certain denominations. For example, we see in the news that many Catholic priests have been charged with child molestation. I am not against Catholic priests, you understand; I am merely trying to get you to understand that they need to recognize this is a spirit from hell that is assigned against them and their work.

When you don't teach people truth, you open the door for bondage, and this is a spirit from hell. The way to get rid of it is for them to get together and say, "This is a spirit that has been assigned to destroy us." Then they need to consecrate themselves to God and cast it out in Jesus' Name.

## Blind to the Enemy

Sometimes we get bitter and angry, and we allow the enemy to make us blind to the forces that have come against our life.

A certain television evangelist said he remembers the day when the spirit that destroyed his life attached itself to him. He was 13 years old, and from that day until the day of his great public fall, he battled that spirit. It would come for a season and then leave, and he would think he was free. Then it would come for another season.

When a spirit is identified, it may manifest itself totally. This happened in the case of a young woman who got involved with a prominent minister. She was known to have a spirit of Jezebel, a spirit of a harlot, long before she became

31

notorious. Rather than repenting of it and being set free, she harbored this unclean spirit, and it manifested itself totally.

We should pray for people caught up in these situations, that God would have mercy on them and set them free.

# Chapter 4

# Your Defense Against Spiritual Assassins

You have a defense against spiritual assassins. You don't have to become a victim of spiritual assassins!

I used to place a lot of emphasis on the altar experience, and I still believe it is important for people to make a public confession for Christ and for people to lay hands on them. However, I have found as a pastor and from studying the Word of God that, as important as the altar experience is, it is equally important that you get some kind of *discipline* to maintain your *deliverance*. If you will not discipline your life, you will need to be delivered again.

I have found that a person with the greatest healing ministry can come to town and pray for you to be healed, but if you walk out of his meeting and remain ignorant of God's covenant of healing and how you got sick in the first place, sooner or later you'll probably need to be prayed for again.

You can give to God and see Him honor His Word and release a financial harvest into your life, but if you don't get teaching and discipline in the way you handle your credit cards and use your money, you will soon be in that same hole again.

I believe the altar experience is important. Although we need to lay hands on people and break demonic powers off them, and although we need to set the sick free from the powers of infirmity and the oppressed from the power of the devil, we must give priority to strong teaching and discipleship to produce lasting freedom.

## What Is Your Destiny?

After the altar experience is when we're going to find out whether your "house" is going to stand. *The destiny of a house is determined by the spirit that is in it.*

My "house" may not look like much. (I'm referring to my natural house — the physical body I live in.) You may look rough on the outside, but if you've got the right spirit on the inside, your destiny is going to be blessed.

On the other hand, you can look all put together on the outside, but if you've got the devil on the inside, you're going to have the devil's destiny on the inside. Again, the destiny of a house is determined by the spirit within it. With that in mind, let us look at Matthew 12, where Jesus said:

> **When the unclean spirit is gone out of a man, he walketh through dry places, seeking rest, and findeth none.**
> **Then he** [the spirit] **saith, I will return into my house from whence I came out....**
>
> **Matthew 12:43,44**

We see, then, a spiritual principle. What you fought once, you will fight again. Maybe you weren't warned about this, and now you wonder why you're having such a battle. Whatever you battled with before you got saved, sooner or later that same spirit is going to return and knock on the door of your house again.

## The Old Demon Pays a Visit

You may be excited about attending church, studying the Word of God, and attending prayer meetings, but down the road there will come a knock on the door. That old demon who once oppressed you will say, "I heard you're still living around here. I came to see if you've still got the same doors unlocked so I can get in the same way I got in the first time."

It is really good when the devil knocks on the door to your house, and *the Holy Spirit* answers! It's also good if the devil comes to your house, kicks the door open, and finds you sitting in there with a shotgun in your hands, loaded up in the Holy Spirit, wearing the full armor of God!

Sometimes people think that just because they prayed a little prayer at an altar, everything is going to be all right. I've seen a lot of people shout and dance and say, "Everything is going to be all right." But a few weeks later, nothing is going right for them, because the condition of that house remains the same.

Our text continues:

> ...and when he is come, he findeth it empty, swept, and garnished.
> Then goeth he, and taketh with himself seven other spirits more wicked than himself, and they enter in and dwell there and the last state of that man is worse than the first. Even so shall it be also unto this wicked generation.
>
> **Matthew 12:44,45**

## Don't Play With Deliverance

Deliverance is not something to be played with. If people don't have sound teaching on the subject, they can end up worse than they were originally.

Some people get set free in church, but you never see them again. You shouldn't come to church to be set free from a spirit if you are not serious about serving God. If you return to your old lifestyle, sooner or later that same spirit is going to return to you.

Notice that the devil doesn't return to your empty house right away. However, when he returns, he says, "This place is empty. The preacher cast out everything that was unclean. Now it's clean in here. It's swept. You've even put a new suit on." You're empty, garnished, and religious looking.

The Bible says that spirit gets other spirits, more wicked than himself, to come back with him, "and the last state of that man is worse than the first."

*The condition your house is in when the spirit attacks you determines your outcome.*

If you are weak when a battle hits, you are in trouble. That's why the Bible says you should always have on the whole armor of God. You should always be ready to resist the devil.

Of course, sometimes you feel stronger than at other times. There are times when you don't feel so strong, but you keep right on going. Why is it that at other times when you don't feel strong, you get beaten up by the devil? It has to do with the condition your house is in when you are attacked. The condition of your house when the unclean spirit attacks you determines your outcome.

I want to warn you concerning the days in which we live. It is not a good time for you to have an in-and-out, up-and-down kind of relationship with God, because the devil is going to be standing there waiting for you to have one of those "down-and-out" days. He wants to catch you out and keep you out!

## The Importance of a Good Foundation

Another important point to understand is: *The foundation of your house determines its destiny.*

Jesus talked about several kinds of houses. He said one house was built on sand, and another was built on the rock. When the test came, the house that was built on the sand fell.

The cold, hard fact of it is: If you have adversity in life, and you give up on God and fall, it's because you didn't have the right foundation. You can blame it on a preacher, misspent money, unmet expectations, or the fact that you got offended, but the truth remains, if you quit because of an adversity, you had the wrong foundation.

Many people say, "I *would* go to church, but I got hurt in church once." No, what happened to you was, the wind came, and the adversary caught you standing on the wrong foundation. I don't care if everyone goes crazy and acts strange; I'm going to keep on serving God. The actions of others have no bearing on my foundation.

You should feel the same way about me. You should say, "Pastor Pitts, we love you, and we're praying for you. But if you go off the deep end, we're still serving God." *Your foundation must be the Word of God.*

Remember, the foundation of your house determines the destiny of your house. It's important that once you're born again, you get involved in a class for new believers. In fact, you should always be in the process of learning, building, and strengthening that foundation so you will remain strong.

## What Name Is Over Your House?

Another point to remember is: *The name over your house has a lot to do with the destiny of that house.*

Joshua said, "As for me and my house, we will serve the Lord." This reminds me of a flag. In history, great houses or castles flew a flag that had their coat of arms on it. Even today, when the Queen of England is in residence in one of her castles, her coat of arms is flown above the building.

When the United States sent astronauts to the moon, the first thing they did was pull out an American flag and plant it in the ground, a gesture that said, "This territory is under the dominion and authority of the United States of America."

So when you become born again, you need to pull down the old flag that was flying above your house, lift up a new flag that proclaims the Name of the Lord Jesus Christ, and declare, "As for me and this house, we will serve the Lord!"

This is meaningful. If you fly a flag, it means that before anyone gets to your castle, they know whom the inhabitants serve.

Your unsaved friends should no longer be able to bring their booze, drugs, immorality, and strife into your house. A new flag is flying — the old administration is out, and the King of kings has come in!

37

## Your Defense Against Assassins

So the flag that is flown over the house is the Name of the Lord. And Proverbs 18:10 states, "The name of the Lord is a strong tower: the righteous runneth into it, and is safe." This refers to your defense against spiritual assassins. *Your defense is the Name of the Lord.* It is a strong tower, and the righteous run into it and are safe.

This tells us that just *being* righteous is not good enough. Many righteous people are being taken out, or killed. You can be righteous and be wrong. You can be righteous and be ignorant. You can be righteous and be *dead!*

So it's not good enough simply to be righteous. This verse says that the righteous *run* into the Name of the Lord. If the righteous don't get under the covering of the Word of God and what His Name means, they're not safe. God's Name means His character, nature, and authority — that's what we run into.

*In a time of trouble, we run into the character, the nature, and the protection of God, and we are safe within the Name of the Lord.* As David said, "He is my strong tower from the enemy" (Psalm 61:3).

Philippians 2:9-11 says:

**Wherefore God also hath highly exalted him, and given him a name which is above every name:**

**That at the name of Jesus every knee should bow, of things in heaven, and things in earth, and things under the earth;**

**And that every tongue should confess that Jesus Christ is Lord, to the glory of God the Father.**

Those demons have to bow — sickness has to bow — when I run into the Name of the Lord. The Name of the Lord is a strong tower!

When you feel like you're about to be assassinated — when you feel like there's trouble on every side — don't run to the telephone or to some person. Run to the Name of the

Lord, and let Him be a strong tower for you! Let His Name be a protection for you. Let His name keep you.

Confess His name, saying, "You are Jehovah-Jireh, the One who meets my need. You are Jehovah-Shammah, the Lord who is present. You are Jehovah-El Shaddai, the Lord who is more than enough." As you confess each name of the Lord, you are building a tower of strength in your life, fortifying yourself from the plan of the enemy. The Name of the Lord really is a strong tower!

In Psalm 61:3, David said, "For thou hast been a shelter for me, and a strong tower from the enemy." The Lord is not just any tower; He is a *strong* tower. We run into His Name, and we are safe.

## Do You Really Have the Lord's Name?

*The revelation of your house determines the destiny or condition of your house.*

**Not every one that saith unto me, Lord, Lord, shall enter into the kingdom of heaven; but he that doeth the will of my Father which is in heaven.**

**Many will say to me in that day, Lord, Lord, have we not prophesied in thy name? and in thy name have cast out devils? and in thy name done many wonderful works?**

**And then will I profess unto them, I never knew you: depart from me, ye that work iniquity.**

**Matthew 7:21-23**

## What Is Your Relationship With Jesus?

The most important things about serving God are not the rules and regulations; but rather, the *relationship*.

You can talk about all the Sunday School classes you attended, how much money you gave to the church, and the positions you have held, but if, in the end, you don't know Jesus, His Name is not over you!

39

Churches are filled with people who think they know the Lord. But if you were to ask the Lord, He would say, "I haven't talked to him for a long time. I don't 'know' him (i.e., we don't have a relationship)."

*Revelation comes by relationship. The revelation of your house determines the destiny or the condition of that house. And revelation is a product of relationship.*

That means you can't manipulate the things of God by getting a "formula" or a "program." The only thing that activates the Word of God is having a personal relationship with the One who wrote the Word. It is not enough to know the Word of God; you *also* must know the God who wrote the Word.

Because I know the character and the nature of the God who wrote the Word, when I read His words to me, it produces a revelation that empowers me to activate His Word.

## Don't Copy Someone Else's Anointing

The things of God come by revelation, not observation and imitation. For example, in Acts 19 the seven sons of Sceva observed Paul casting out devils. They were observing to find a formula, like many people do today. We observe an anointed servant of God, and we watch *how* he does it. Why? Because we want to do "it" like he does it.

Our observation brings us into imitation. We then become more concerned with mannerisms, voice inflections, hairdos, suits, and ties than we do with the revelation which brought that individual to a place of prominence.

After observing Paul, the Sceva brothers decided to try their hand at it. I can hear them say, "Let's find someone who's demon possessed."

If you think about it, it is interesting to realize that you don't have to be "deep" to know someone is demon possessed. Why is it that church people don't believe in demons, yet the seven sons of Sceva, who weren't in a relationship with the Lord, said, "We know we can find someone who's demon possessed."

Sure enough, before long they found someone who was possessed, and they got out their notes and began imitating the works of Paul. The brothers grabbed their victim and said to him, "In the Name of Jesus who Paul preaches about, come out of him!"

## Jesus I Know; But Who Are You?

The Bible says this demon spoke, "Jesus I know, and Paul I know; *but who are you?*" (Acts 19:15).

Now these seven brothers were in bad shape. If they were to go to heaven and stand before the Lord, He would say, "You've got to depart from Me, because I don't know you."

After the devil said, "Who are you?" the Bible says the demon beat the seven brothers so severely that they went running home naked and wounded.

This story tells us that you can try to use a method someone else has, but if you don't have the revelation behind it, you will fail.

People may come to a certain city and declare, "We're going to take this city!" However, if they don't have the revelation of how to do it, they will not be effective against its principalities. There is a great truth here: Don't try to copy someone and use something if you don't have the anointing behind it!

## Have Intercessors Build Your Moat

*The relationships of your house affect its outcome.* One of your protections against spiritual assassins is your intercessors. We're referring to building a spiritual house or tower right now, the Name of the Lord being that strong tower.

I always picture intercessors as digging the moat that surrounds the castle. Everyone ought to have some intercessors pray a moat around their castle. This means, before the devil can even get up on your front porch, he's got to wade through a moat filled with the blood of Jesus!

41

This doesn't mean you need to sit in your house all day and intercede for each other. And it doesn't mean you should tell your friends all your deep, dark secrets. You shouldn't be confessing "down;" you should be confessing "up" to people of higher spiritual authority.

Don't tell people all of your problems; especially when you are not sure how strong they are. If they've got lots of problems themselves, before you know it, the devil will make a ruin out of both of you!

A man and a woman in a certain church began praying together. He said, "You know, I have to confess, I've been lusting after you."

She said, "Oh, no! I've been lusting after you, too." You know the end of that story. Sad to say, things like that have happened.

An unmarried couple in the church were always going off by themselves. Someone warned them, "You shouldn't be going off by yourselves alone all the time." They ignored the advice, saying, "We're just studying the Bible together." The next thing we knew, the girl turned up pregnant.

I asked them, "What happened to you? I thought you were studying the Bible."

## Associate With Intercessors

The importance of good relationships is discussed in Ecclesiastes 4:9,10:

**Two are better than one; because they have a good reward for their labour.**

**For if they fall, the one will lift up his fellow: but woe to him that is alone when he falleth; for he hath not another to help him up.**

It is not a coincidence that when Jesus anointed His disciples, He sent them out two by two.

When you walk through this life, you need to have some intercessors, friends, and associates by your side. If the people you deal with always leave you more depressed than when you began your relationship, find people who can help you.

So the relationships of your house are very important. It is said, "A person (or house) is known by the company he keeps." Here is a question for you: Why do all those demonized people feel so good coming to your house? Why can't you get those gossipy people to leave your house? Why do they feel at home there? Just wondering....

So we see one of the ways to be free from spiritual assassins is being around intercessors. Everyone ought to know intercessors who will keep you free from the spiritual assassins set on assignment against you.

If you have a nasty spirit, you'll be uncomfortable around intercessors. If they are spiritually in tune when you approach them and you've got a wrong spirit, they may let you know about it. They may not even say anything; they may just look at you in such a way as to let you know they know the score.

As we pointed out earlier, when the devil gets ready to assassinate you, he will seek to get you away from such people.

## The Role of Ushers and Greeters

Ushers and greeters should intercede for the house of God, praying and working for God's Spirit to be there.

Sometimes people who come into the house of God have unclean spirits attached to them. I don't want you to think that everyone has a demon, but sometimes people come in who are bound up by something.

If you're an usher or a greeter, you don't have to make a big deal over it when such people come. You don't need to call out happily to the other greeters, "Come here! We've got *a live one* over here — one with all kinds of spirits!"

You should operate in the right spirit and discernment, patting such a person on the shoulder and saying softly, "In the Name of Jesus...." The way you shake that person's hand

and the way you minister to him or her may make the difference between someone who will give their heart to the Lord, or someone who will go home that day and beat their children.

## Be Led by the Holy Spirit

You need to have discernment and know what you're doing in the house of God. You need to know how to minister in each particular environment and church. For example, our church in Toledo is not a formal church with a planned program we can hand you. There isn't always a set format in a Spirit-filled church. We are led by the Holy Spirit.

You may know all the old songs, but God may want to give us a new song, so you'll actually have to concentrate and flow in the "spirit" of the song instead of just singing the words by rote memory.

You must be led by the Spirit to be part of a Spirit-filled church like ours. The church I pastor is not a comfortable place where we do the same old thing every time we meet, because we're battling for the soul of our city.

That means we've got to be led by the Spirit; we've got to flow in the Spirit; we've got to learn to fight in the Spirit; and we've got to develop an attitude that *likes* to fight the devil.

Remember the kids in your school whom you didn't want to fight because they liked to fight? Everyone stayed away from them because they *loved* a good fight. They looked forward to it. And that's the way you've got to be in the Holy Spirit.

Then the devil will say, "Stay away from those people, because they love to fight and win!"

## Chapter 5

# Bread, Wine, and a Kid

*A*nointed *music will definitely break spirits off people.* Here is scripture to back this up.

But the Spirit of the Lord departed from Saul, and an evil spirit from the Lord troubled him.

And Saul's servants said unto him, Behold now, an evil spirit from God troubleth thee.

Let our lord now command thy servants, which are before thee, to seek out a man, who is a cunning player on an harp: and it shall come to pass, when the evil spirit from God is upon thee, that he shall play with his hand, and thou shalt be well.

And Saul said unto his servants, Provide me now a man that can play well, and bring him to me.

Then answered one of the servants, and said, Behold, I have seen a son of Jesse the Bethlehemite, that is cunning in playing, and a mighty valiant man, and a man of war, and prudent in matters, and a comely person, and the Lord is with him.

Wherefore Saul sent messengers unto Jesse, and said, Send me David thy son, which is with the sheep.

And Jesse took an ass laden with bread, and a bottle of wine, and a kid, and sent them by David his son unto Saul.

**1 Samuel 16:14-20**

Verse 20 is especially important for those of you who are involved in the public praise and worship ministry.

45

## The Father's Provision

Notice that before he came to minister — before he came to deliver Saul from his evil spirit — David was provided by his father with bread, wine, and a kid.

*The bread speaks to us of a revelation of the Word of God.* Man shall not live by bread alone, but by every word that proceedeth out of the mouth of God. If you are going to minister to people and set them free in music, you must have a revelation of what you are singing. *It must be real to you!*

This also holds true for members of the congregation.

Some people get caught up in the music — the beat or the style — and miss the anointing of God, because they don't have a revelation of what they're singing.

*The wine speaks to us of the Holy Spirit.* If you are going to set someone else free, you must be filled with the Holy Spirit and have the anointing of God upon your life. Your talent, ability, voice, or public expression will not deliver someone in the realm of the spirit. You must have the anointing to do this.

*The kid speaks of sacrifice.* You can never do anything for God until you are willing to sacrifice yourself to set someone else free. It takes sacrifice. No matter what ministry you're going to be involved in, a certain amount of sacrifice is involved.

There's a sacrifice of time, a sacrifice to practice, or a sacrifice to shut yourself away from the cares of the world and go to a quiet place to hear from God.

This also speaks of public sacrifice. You cannot lead people into a public sacrifice until you have experienced your own personal sacrifice. Notice that David's father gave David his own kid. *Everyone must make his own sacrifice to the Lord.* The story continues in verse 21:

## The Love That Sets Men Free

**And David came to Saul, and stood before him: and he loved him greatly....**

This is also noteworthy. *You cannot set someone free whom you do not love. You cannot win a city that you do not love.* Don't come around me telling me how bad my city is, because I'll tell you to leave my presence until you go pray for this city. I love this city.

You can't win a city until you love it. You can't win a city unless you love the people in it. And you can't win your family unless you love your family.

David loved Saul. It didn't mean that Saul was faultless; David loved him anyway.

**And David came to Saul, and stood before him: and he loved him greatly; and he became his armourbearer.**

**And Saul sent to Jesse, saying, Let David, I pray thee, stand before me; for he hath found favour in my sight.**

**And it came to pass, when the evil spirit from God was upon Saul, that David took an harp, and played with his hand: so Saul was refreshed, and was well, and the evil spirit departed from him.**

**1 Samuel 16:21-23**

There is an anointing that comes upon the atmosphere by worship and praise when God's people have a revelation of what they're singing; when they have an anointing from the One to whom they are singing; and when they are making sacrifice.

Such a powerful anointing comes that people who are bound by spirits will be set free! The very music, attitude, and worship they are experiencing will begin to reverberate on the inside of them until the spirits have to loose their hold and come out!

## How To Minister

Everyone, especially musicians, must learn how to worship God in the spirit. There's a way to worship God upon the drums that will drive spirits out of people. There's a right sound and a right time upon the keyboards that will release the anointing. There's a right song at the right time. There are also wrong songs at the wrong time.

*A Spirit-filled church must not minister, move, play, or deliver the anointing out of their own emotional realm, or out of the people's preconceived preference for music style.*

Instead, we must minister out of a spiritual relationship; out of a love for God and people. We must announce, "We're going to bring God's presence down until you are set free by the power of God!"

## The Transferable Anointing

Remember this: *The only anointing that is transferable is a tangible one.*

You can be prayed for by a lot of people and never receive a tangible deposit of the anointing. There are other times, however, when there is a heavy anointing upon a person, a meeting, or a church until people know it!

Many people have walked into one of our services and said, "There's something different here." Often it's because there is a tangible anointing — an anointing you can sense.

During one Thursday night service, a strong anointing of God was on me, and I prayed for many people. The service lasted until late at night, and I was physically drained, yet the tangible anointing of God filled the church and remained on me. It was still on me the next day, when I went to a local mall. I was dressed in casual clothes, wearing a ball cap, just walking around.

Later, one of the young men of the church told his parents that he had seen me there. "When I saw Pastor Pitts in the mall," he said, "my insides began to shake. The rest of the day, I wanted to cry."

When you have a tangible anointing like this, it is transferable. When there's an anointing upon you, and you get in the presence of someone else, it jumps on them. You feel it reverberating in your spirit. It runs up and down your arms. It gets into your spirit — into your mind — into your very being. When you get into that anointing, you don't always want to go out with a bunch of people after the service; you want to go home and seek God. It's a tangible anointing, the *shekinah* glory of God.

It is the only anointing that is transferable, and it brings a responsibility on believers. For example, there is a responsibility on church leaders to seek God so that even if the sound system blows up during the song service, or if a visitor doesn't understand everything about the service, there is still a transferable anointing that gets on them and sets the captives free.

## Covenant or Curse?

**Thou shalt remember the Lord thy God: for it is he that giveth thee power to get wealth, that he may establish his covenant which he sware unto thy fathers, as it is this day.**

**And it shall be, if thou do at all forget the Lord thy God, and walk after other gods, and serve them, and worship them…ye shall surely perish.**

**Deuteronomy 8:18,19**

*The blessing or covenant of the house determines its destiny.*
You can defend yourself against spiritual assassins by your giving. This is amazing, but many are not being set free, according to Malachi, because they're under a curse!

**Will a man rob God? Yet ye have robbed me. But ye say, Wherein have we robbed thee? In tithes and offerings.**

*Ye are cursed with a curse:* **for ye have robbed me, even this whole nation.**

**Malachi 3:8,9**

If there are gangsters in your family or in your city, they can bring a curse upon you. For cities to be blessed, prayers must be made for people in organized crime to be saved and for the city's finances to be loosed.

We don't talk about them too much anymore, but there are a lot of mobsters in cities — racketeers, gangsters, people

who give bribes, and people who take advantage of the oppressed — *and they have to come down!* They cannot stay.

One way to reverse a curse is to get the blessing flowing.

## Keep Me Covered!

*The covering of the house determines its destiny.*

To build a strong spiritual house, you must not only
have a foundation, walls, fellowship, and relationship — you
also need a roof.

"Covering" speaks of authority. We're in a generation
that does not like to recognize authority, but the Bible plainly
teaches that if you are out from under authority, you are uncovered and unprotected.

Gangsters have a better concept of this than Christian
people. They say, "I'm getting ready to go in there and hit this
store. You keep me covered." What that means is, "If someone starts shooting at me, you've got me covered. "

Yet Christian people don't understand the principle of
covering or authority — *the uncovered environment is an unprotected environment.* That means you should be under
someone of greater authority to be protected in spiritual
warfare.

This is the principle of covering or headship: First
Corinthians 11:3 (*Weymouth*) tells us, "I would have you know
however that of every man, Christ is the Head. That of a
woman her husband is the Head as God is Christ's Head."

We do know that Christ is the *Head* of the Church. God's
kingdom functions in supernatural power when delegated
authority is recognized.

## I Am a Man Under Authority

We can see this principle in a passage from Matthew 8.

**And when Jesus was entered into Capernaum, there came
unto him a centurion, beseeching him,**

And saying, Lord, my servant lieth at home sick of the palsy, grievously tormented.

And Jesus saith unto him, I will come and heal him.

The centurion answered and said, Lord, I am not worthy that thou shouldest come under my roof: but *speak the word only,* and my servant shall be healed.

*For I am a man under authority,* having soldiers under me: and I say to this man, Go, and he goeth; and to another, Come, and he cometh; and to my servant, Do this, and he doeth it.

When Jesus heard it, he marvelled, and said to them that followed, Verily I say unto you, I have not found so great faith, no, not in Israel.

**Matthew 8:5-10**

A centurion is a military man with soldiers under his command. Yet in verse 9 he said, "For I am a man under authority." You, too, are a person under authority.

What the centurion was saying was, "Jesus, I recognize your authority, because I am a person who both has and is under authority. I know that my authority comes from those who are over me in the military. They have given me authority over those who are under me. I can say to one of the privates, 'You go over there,' and without any back talk, he goes. And I can tell another soldier, 'You come here,' and without questioning why, he comes."

## Speak the Word Only

"Jesus, I have that kind of authority, so I know You have that authority, too. I know You can tell the ministering angels to go, and they will go without questioning. Therefore, You don't even need to come to my house. Speak the word only, and my servant will be healed."

Jesus looked at this man and said, "I have not seen so great a faith, no, not in Israel" (verse 10). Jesus said this centurion had the most faith of anyone He had ever met, because he was a person who recognized authority!

51

The problem with a lot of people is, they don't have any covering. They are not under any authority. They run here, there, and everywhere. They are not under anyone's teaching.

No one can tell them anything, because they think they know as much as everyone, and no one is spiritual enough to teach them anything.

Therefore, when the devil comes, they say, "Go!" but he replies, "I'm not going anywhere." They say to the angels, "Come!" and the angels say, "We're not coming." The kingdom of God operates based on authority.

The whole Church needs teaching like this. Understanding and operating under authority will make us strong.


## Not Forsaking the Assembling of Ourselves

We need to get the Word deep inside, words like those found in Hebrews 10:25:

**Not forsaking the assembling of ourselves together, as the manner of some is; but exhorting one another: and so much the more, as ye see the day approaching.**

Some people don't have a home church, don't want a church, and don't need a church — they think.

That was a problem back in New Testament days, too. Paul said, "We are not forsaking the assembling of ourselves together, as the manner of some is." The next phrase says, "So much the more, as you see the day approaching." This means that the more evil and wicked the times get, the more we need to get together, not *less*! We need to free our schedules so we can assemble with the saints of God.

Now I'm going to take us a step further here. Notice that word "assembled." There's a difference between all being in the same building and being "assembled." The church does not have authority just because everyone shows up; the church has authority when we are "assembled."

## Some Assembly Required

Not long ago, I bought some bicycles. They came in boxes, and it said on the box, "Some assembly required." That's what a lot of churches are like: All the parts are there, but they're not *assembled* — they're not put together. The difference in a New Testament church is, we expect you to get assembled when you come in!

Much of what is going on in the church world today is really *rebellion*. When you cannot find a church that is spiritual enough for you, you are rebellious, and someone ought to tell you so. When you are always at odds with authority figures, you are rebellious.

You can't be delivered when you're in that position. The Bible says, "Rebellion is as the sin of witchcraft" (1 Samuel 15:23). If you are in rebellion, before we can deliver you, you must repent for your rebellion.

You and I both know there are many people today in the church world who are uncovered, having Bible studies and little prayer groups that meet in their homes without any covering or permission from a pastor or a church. They have self-appointed and self-anointed themselves, and they often are suddenly destroyed because they are uncovered.

The real bottom line is: Someone wouldn't let them do their thing, or someone preached on their pet sin, and they got offended. They carry that offense until it produces rebellion, oftentimes never submitting to authority. Thus, they are open for assassination because they have no covering.

## Petty Differences

One of the principal tactics the devil uses to assassinate you is getting you at odds with your covering. People will act "spiritual" about something petty and carnal, not knowing the enemy is actually behind it.

Many people in the kingdom of God do things I don't understand; however, it is not my job to talk against them. I didn't call them, and I can't "un-call" them. I didn't anoint them, and I can't "un-anoint" them.

When people come to my church, I tell them, "Don't come here talking bad about someone else." A disrespectful attitude is the channel the devil will flow through to destroy you! If you have no respect for someone, you cannot receive or be taught by the anointing of God that is in them.

## Beware the Root of Bitterness

The Bible warns us to beware, "...lest any root of bitterness springing up trouble you, and thereby many be defiled" (Hebrews 12:15). Notice it doesn't say "a tree," or even "a manifestation" of bitterness. So be careful that you don't let even the root get started, because there will always be someone ready to come by and "water" it for you.

They will say, "You saw how the pastor walked right past you on Sunday. He doesn't care about folks anymore." Yet they just threw a seed in your spirit, and now you're going home believing that the pastor God gave you doesn't care about anyone.

You say to yourself, "He sure doesn't. He comes in the service late, prays for a lot of people, and leaves. I tried to shake his hand, but the ushers wouldn't let me. He doesn't care about anyone."

Your rebellion can start this innocently and easily. You never stop to think that your pastor preached and then prayed for hundreds of people under the anointing of the Holy Spirit in that service, and he was being ushered to a place of recuperation.

## The Seed of Rebellion Grows

If a little seed of rebellion gets started the wrong way, all of a sudden it becomes a wall. Now, when everyone else is receiving, you're not. But rather than admitting it's rebellion, suddenly something is wrong with everyone else.

You complain, "The pastor used to preach fine, but now he doesn't flow. Have you noticed that the anointing has lifted off him?"

That's a sure sign you're ready to be assassinated. You can develop your little attitude until you miss God totally while everyone else keeps going on, shouting and praising God.

We will deal more directly with this important area later in the book, but let me state here that there is safety when you are accountable and under the authority of a godly pastor.

When God gifts you with a spiritual covering, value it, support it, pray and intercede for the success of it, and do not allow spiritual assassins to separate you.

# Chapter 6

# The Road of No Return

*...for wide is the gate, and broad is the way, that leadeth to destruction, and many there be which go in thereat.*

**Matthew 7:13**

H ave you ever wondered why some people are not delivered? There are even those who sit in the church, answer altar calls, and say all the right things, but somehow you are aware that there is something not right with them.

They say they want to do right. They may even cry and become emotional, yet all you know is you are not "buying" it. When you pray for them, you sense a resistance — some kind of shell around them — which renders your prayers, the pastor's message, and the counsel of friends useless.

There are people today who, in their present state, *cannot* be delivered! This is a chilling thought, although true nonetheless. It is possible to come to the place where God takes His hand off you. Some are there now, and some are heading that way to their destination of destruction, which I call "the road of no return."

## God Gives Up on Some People

Let's look at a portion of Romans 1:24: "Wherefore God also *gave them up*...." Then look at verse 26: "For this cause God *gave them up*...." And verse 32: "Who knowing the judgment of God, that they which commit such things are worthy of death, not only do the same, but have pleasure in them that do them."

We don't need to go into all the details or the *exegesis* of that portion of scripture; the important thing to see from it is that *it is possible for God to give up on some people!*

Now let's go back to a story in the Old Testament. First Samuel 16 tells us about a man named Saul. Saul was chosen by God to rule over Israel, but eventually he began to rely on his past relationship with God. *It's important for you to know that just because you once had something with God doesn't mean that you still possess it today.*

In First Samuel 16:14, we read, "But the Spirit of the Lord departed from Saul, and an evil spirit from the Lord troubled him."

## King Saul's Road of No Return

"And Saul's servants said unto him, Behold now, an evil spirit from God troubleth thee" (verse 15). Reading this portion of scripture, you find how King Saul got to the place where he began on the "road of no return."

Some people don't believe that the Spirit of God can leave you, but that's exactly what happened to Saul; and that's why I'm sharing this message with you — the message that you *can* come to a place where you make God weary of dealing with you!

This message needs to be brought to people who have sat in church service after church service after church service, yet they have hardened their hearts against every altar call and every preacher they have ever heard. They have said to themselves, "I'll get saved some day when *I'm ready* to get saved."

Someone needs to tell them, "Just because you want to get saved *some day* doesn't mean you are going to be able to get saved *on that day*. God can become wearied with you. And when God has had enough of your insolence, He's going to take His hand off you and turn you over to that evil spirit you've been playing with for your destruction!"

We see this throughout the Word of God. It is a sad and sobering message. Nevertheless, it is *true* that when God gets tired of dealing with you, you're going to be one sorry individual.

## The Fear of the Lord

There are people sitting in churches today who have lost their fear of God. Many preachers have tried to paint God as some kind of a cosmic "teddy bear" or "big brother" with clout whose job is to follow you around and make sure everything comes out all right for you.

God has another side that is not talked much about, and that is that He is holy. When God is refused and rejected, and when mortals into whom God has breathed the breath of life shake their fist in His face and shout, "I won't do what You tell me to do! I won't serve You!" God can become angry with you.

The Bible says in Hebrews 10:31, "It is a fearful thing to fall into the hands of the living God." You only *think* you have trouble when your wife gets angry at you; you're going to know what *real* trouble is when God gets angry at you! When God has had enough, He takes His hand of protection off you, and He allows that spirit you've been playing with to control you.

## Nebuchadnezzar Goes Insane

This happened to King Nebuchadnezzar after he hardened his heart against God. God told him, "You're full of pride. You're taking credit for what I did for you." So God took His hand off the once-mighty king and turned him over to spirits of insanity.

For seven years the king roamed the fields like a beast, "...and did eat grass as oxen...till his hairs were grown like eagles' feathers, and his nails like birds' claws" (Daniel 4:33). People pointed to him and asked, "What kind of an animal is that over there?" and they had to say, "That's Nebuchadnezzar. He used to be king, but God turned him over to evil spirits."

After seven years, Nebuchadnezzar was restored to his right mind, humbly gave God all the glory, and assumed his kingly duties once again.

Unfortunately, his son, Belshazzar, didn't learn anything from Nebuchadnezzar's lesson. One night after Belshazzar had become king, he was holding a large, boisterous party in his palace, and he drunkenly called for the gold and silver vessels his father had removed from God's Temple in Jerusalem. He and his thousand guests began to drink out of the holy vessels and to use them to worship other gods.

Everything was going just the way Belshazzar wanted — but then God crashed his party! God wrote on the wall with His finger, and the words were interpreted by Daniel to mean, "This night you have been weighed in the balance, and you have been found wanting. This night your kingdom is taken away from you!"

The king's knees began to shake, and he sobered up in a hurry, but it was too late! He was slain that night, and his kingdom was given to the Medes and the Persians. (See Daniel 5.)

## Man Cannot Manipulate God

I want to remind you that God is still in control. I want to remind you that just because you serve God doesn't mean you can manipulate Him and tell Him to do whatever you want Him to do. The reason our churches are weak and infirm and we have lost authority in our communities is because people are trying to manipulate God and are refusing to allow God to be Supreme.

I want to declare to you that God is sending "preachers of righteousness" back into the Church who are going to stand and declare the Word of Almighty God. God is going to raise up preachers who aren't concerned about religious politics. God is going to raise up people who can't be bought off, controlled, manipulated, or intimidated — people who don't care about your opinion, your mama's opinion, your daddy's opinion, or your denomination's opinion. God is not moved by what you think!

## Don't Turn on God's Messenger

Since God is faithful, He will send someone your way to challenge your religious way of thinking which causes you to think you can get by with manipulating God. God would like you to remember that He is the Creator; you are the creation — and you can't fight Him and win.

There are too many people in churches who have problems with every preacher they have ever heard. They are in rebellion against every church they have ever been in. They fight the move of God whenever and wherever they find it. If you are like this, *today* is your day to repent before God takes His hands off you and allows you to go down the road of no return.

When King Saul was in this position, he called for David, an anointed man of God. As David began to play upon his harp, it drove the evil spirit away from Saul. But then something ominous happened: Saul became jealous and developed a hatred for David.

Every reference I have found in the Bible about God's turning someone over to the devil is preceded by the fact that these people developed an attitude toward the godly persons God had sent to warn and deliver them.

## How Do You Treat God's Representative?

I learned that God had never turned anyone over to the devil without first sending a godly person to them. When they turned against that godly person, God took His hands off them, because *the way you treat God's representative is symbolic of how you deal with God Himself.*

After Saul developed a jealous attitude toward David, the evil spirit returned to the king. Again his advisers called for David, pleading, "David, please come and play your harp for the king, because when you play, the evil spirit is driven away from him."

The Bible records that this time when David entered the king's presence, Saul was holding a javelin in his hand. And when David began to play, the evil spirit began to manifest — just like some of you do anytime you get around an anointed man of God with whom you have a problem. No, you may not be holding a physical javelin, but you have a sharp tongue or an attitude problem, and you pick up that "javelin" and throw it.

## Sudden Destruction

*When Saul threw his javelin at David in a murderous rage, the evil spirit came upon him and never left him from that day forward.* There is a price to pay for rebellion. Eventually, King Saul, in the midst of battle, committed suicide by falling on his own sword. (See First Samuel 31.) His three sons died in battle the same day.

There is a price to pay for joining yourself to rebellious people. Saul's armourbearer also committed suicide that day. These men got on the road of no return, and they all died and went into eternity prematurely!

The Bible says in Proverbs 29:1, "He, that being *often reproved* hardeneth his neck, shall suddenly be destroyed, and that *without remedy*." Some people are walking on dangerous ground, because God has sent people to warn them about their rebellious ways and attitudes, yet they refuse to heed these rebukes and warnings!

## Consequences of Killing God's Prophets and Apostles

The Bible is clear that the reason Israel was judged was because God had sent them prophets, but they killed them. He had sent them John the Baptist, but they killed him. He had sent them the 12 apostles of the Lamb, but they martyred all but John. And God said, "I'm taking my hand off you, and I'm turning you over to your enemies!"

Some people have been witnessed to and prayed for by many messengers from God. While they were praying for you and witnessing to you, you were running them down and fighting them. If you fight the things of God, you are in danger of heading down *the road of no return.* Today is your day to stop — repent — turn round — and be delivered.

The Lord put a word in my heart that He was going to send to our church people who are *too bent over to stand up,* people who have been *too stubborn to submit,* and people who have been *too bruised to get healed* — and that a three-pronged word was going to be in my mouth. It was going to be a word of *deliverance,* a word of *healing,* and a word of *restoration.* The Lord told me that the word would be strong, but not to hold back on it — to loose it and let it go — because it would save people's souls!

I believe that anointing is also on the words I write. They are strong, but they will bring deliverance! Don't get me wrong — I believe God is good, but we have attached our definition of "good" to God. When we say God is a *"good"* God, that doesn't mean He's good like *we're* good; it means He's good like *He's* good.

When God sends rebuke to us, it doesn't mean He is not good; but, rather, what we are doing is not good. Don't confuse God's correction as meaning something is wrong with God. We have become so arrogant, we won't serve God *His* way; we insist on serving Him our way.

Our cities no longer fear God, because God's people no longer fear Him. There was a day in this country when there was such a reverence and a fear of God that drunkards and fornicators would cross the street to keep from walking in front of a church. That kind of fear is good.

Now we don't need to go out in the streets to find sinners — the drunkards are on the deacon board, and the fornicators are in the choir! They'll sit at a club all Saturday night, come to church on Sunday, and sing like they own the place. Having no fear of God and resisting God's correction, they are fast on the road of no return.

Somehow we think we are getting away with something. We think God doesn't know about us. I challenge the rebellious: Consider what is going to happen to you when God takes His hand off you. Your bank account can't protect you. The Communion line you went through won't protect you. All the little relics you've put in your house won't help you once you start down the road of no return.

God help us, there are so many people on the road of no return! They could get to the place of Nebuchadnezzar, Belshazzar, and other Bible characters — the place where God has to take His hand off them when they will no longer receive the correction of the Lord.

We've become so comfort-oriented in the modern church that many Christians have lost this awful truth. They are used to someone patting their flesh, tickling their ears, and making them feel they are right when they are wrong. They think there's something wrong with the preacher, but God is not moved by their denominational affiliations or their unbelieving attitudes.

The purpose of this teaching is not to make Christians happy; it is *to save souls from hell!* This may be someone's last chance to be confronted with this warning. There will come a day when it is the last time they will hear God call their name.

They told God, "Get away from me! Get away from me!" and one day He is going to go away from them. Then they are going to want Him to come back and seek them, but God is going to leave them and write *Ichabod* (meaning "the glory has departed") above the door of their house.

Many have been sitting around playing church, feeling good, and losing the battle. Every year in America, 6,000 to 7,000 churches close permanently because of the divisions in them. This spirit of rebellion needs to be broken and cast out of people in the Name of Jesus. It needs to be dealt with publicly until people come to order, and conviction, glory, and joy return to the house of God.

Some people run from church to church, causing problems every place they go — and they have no fear of doing so.

Churches are being destroyed in our city. There is no understanding of order in these houses of God. Everyone is doing his own thing. People are fighting and carrying on — yet they pretend they are proponents of revival! They have lost their witness to the city, and even the sinners know they're unruly! Pastors and members of such churches need to quit praying for revival and deal with the sin in their camp.

## The Roadblock of Rebuke

I found something interesting in the Word of God: Whenever we start down the road of no return, *God sets up a roadblock in our path.* The name of this roadblock is "rebuke."

We don't hear preaching on this anymore, but the fact remains that before you go off on the wrong road, God will send a godly person to you to rebuke you in the Name of Jesus. We all talk about rebuking the devil, but sometimes *people* need to be rebuked.

There's a difference between someone who *disagrees* with you and someone who *rebukes* you. Unfortunately, the people who need to be rebuked often won't receive it.

I found a principle in the Word of God that when you turn on the godly person God has sent to rebuke you, God may very well take His hand off you and say, "Go ahead." By stating this, however, I am not giving you license to run through the church rebuking everyone at your discretion.

God does, however, allow those who have spiritual oversight over you to see things you don't see. Your overseer sees things you don't see. That's why he or she is called "oversight" — they see *over* you. The tenth chapter of John tells us the Good Shepherd sees the wolf *coming* before it gets to the flock.

Obey those who have the rule over you, for they *watch* for your soul. *The real test of submission is not when you see danger; it's how you respond when you do not see it first.*

Let's add another scripture to clarify this: "There is a way which seemeth right unto a man, but the end thereof are the ways of death" (Proverbs 14:12). The reason you have to be rebuked is because you think you are right; *it seems right to you.*

The Body of Christ has been a body that is recklessly out of order. We attend, we visit, we frequent, we worship — but we don't really *join* and *submit.* I believe strongly that when God calls a person to pastor in a place, He also calls the people who should be fed by, watched over, and instructed by that ministry gift.

It is this supernatural process of being guided, guarded, and governed that brings us serenity, security, and success. If you are not under proper authority, you may miss opportunities to hear the Word God meant for you to hear in that church. Don't be like Saul and turn on the very one who comes to deliver you!

We get excited about challenging the spirits and the city, but we have to start by challenging the people. God said of *His* pastors, "I will set them up *over* them" — not beside or under their people, but *over* them. (See Jeremiah 23:4.)

Many people who go to a church disregard teaching and continue to live any way they want. No one ever challenges them as to their manner of life. Confrontation is a powerful tool when exercised under the direction of the Holy Spirit.

The apostle Paul once confronted Elymas, a sorcerer who was filled with the devil. (The man would probably have had a 1-900 number if it had been available then, and he would have gotten some famous backslidden celebrity to be on the program with him!)

Elymas was bound by a spirit and would not let it go. He was influencing officials against the Gospel (Acts 13). Finally Paul denounced him as a son of the devil and a foe to all that is right. At the same time, Paul announced that God was judging Elymas with blindness — and the man went blind on the spot.

I am not trying to propose that we start speaking curses

on people, but, rather, making the point that there is a level of authority in God which baffles the natural mind.

There are times when our political and religious officials need to be rebuked in the Name of God for what they have done to the people whom they are supposed to be serving, but this cannot happen until God's people submit to God themselves. I am not referring to storybook Christianity; I am referring to New Testament revival!

Someone needs to hold the political system, the educational system, and the economic system accountable. But they can be held accountable only when God's people first submit to the truth. *A rebuke can never go through us until it first comes to us.*

It is important that we seek godly authority and then submit and support it. God gets glory out of our relating properly to authority. To see how important this covering is, look at First Timothy 1:18. Paul, writing to Timothy, says:

> **This charge I commit unto thee, son Timothy, according to the prophecies which went before on thee, that thou by them mightest war a good warfare.**

These are words for a church that is going to be in warfare! Paul continues in verses 19 and 20:

> **Holding faith, and a good conscience; which some having put away concerning faith have made shipwreck:**
> **Of whom is Hymenaeus and Alexander; *whom I have delivered unto Satan, that they may learn not to blaspheme.***

Any way you look at it, that's a strong word. Many Bible scholars agree, as do I, that the phrase *"I have delivered over unto Satan"* means "I have put him out of the Church."

In the minds of members of the New Testament Church, if you were put out of the Church, it was the same as handing you over to the devil. This is the principle of excommunication. It can be taken too far, but it is nevertheless within the authority of the Church.

We take our covering so lightly, yet when we are committed and covered, we are postured for promotion.

Examine yourself today. God does not want you controlled, dominated, or manipulated! However, He wants us to be subject to godly authority who speak, instruct, and correct us, that we might be promoted and blessed. Therefore, let us not be self-willed and unteachable, but let us, with a contrite spirit, humbly seek the road less traveled!

**Because strait is the gate, and narrow is the way, which leadeth unto life, and few there be that find it.**
**Matthew 7:14**

# Chapter 7

# The Godly Rebuke

When it comes to rebuke, you must know when and how to rebuke a person. If you rebuke someone who is just a baby in Christ and doesn't know any better, you could hurt that person. That's not the purpose of rebuke. Rebuke is meant to correct people and bring life to them.

For example, I was ministering at a church once, and a woman got up to sing a special just before I was to preach. She was carnal looking, wearing big go-go boots with real tight pants tucked into them. And as she sang, she gyrated vigorously.

I decided I was going to rebuke her soundly when I got up to preach. I thought, "I'm going to set her straight!" The thing that upset me most was that some men in the congregation were really into it, swaying to the music and to her motions. Men who hadn't praised God all year were shouting, "Sing, Sister, sing!" Another thing that disturbed me was that they didn't understand how serious this offense was to God.

As I started to walk to the pulpit, the Holy Spirit checked me. He said, "No, don't bother her. She is a new convert, and her pastor ought to teach her. Just go on with the service. I'm going to deal with her."

When I got to the pulpit, I asked my wife, Kathi, to come and sing a chorus, because when this woman started doing her thing, the Holy Spirit packed His bags and left. He was *gone*! I hoped He would come back and help us if my godly wife sang under the anointing.

When Kathi began to sing, the anointing of the Lord hit that place! Tears began to stream down the other singer's face, and she ran to the front and repented in front of all of us.

She said, "When I saw the anointing, I realized I was in the flesh and was wrong. I ask you to forgive me for what I have done." God can deal with tenderhearted, teachable people like her. Once she realized she was doing wrong, she quickly repented.


## Time for a Rebuke

Often we know we're wrong, but we don't want to change what we're doing. If you tell someone who is ruining his life, "You shouldn't be doing this," he will probably reply, "I know that's my problem." *We know!* When we know we're wrong, but we won't change, it's time for a rebuke to remind us to get back on the right path.

I'll give you another example. I was in a church recently where the people had a good foundation and solid teaching, yet their musicians were getting carnal. Sometimes musicians get carnal, just like the rest of you get carnal. These had become carnal. They weren't flowing in the Spirit anymore.

I noticed when they had finished doing their thing, they all disappeared through a side door that led into a hallway. I looked for them when I got up to preach, but I still couldn't find any of them. It grieved me to the point I couldn't preach, so I stopped and said, "Where are the musicians?" I just opened it up for a public response.

Finally someone said, "Well, they're out in the hall."

"We'll wait for them," I said. "Go get them."

The whole congregation waited for them. They came tiptoeing back in. They knew they were busted. I just stood there and looked at them. They all sat down.

## A Rebuke to Carnal Musicians

I asked, "Where are your Bibles? Not one of you has a Bible!" I said this in front of the congregation. I had an anointing for rebuke.

I continued, "Not one of you has a Bible — *not one of you!* That's why you're so carnal! The Lord shows me you've been sitting around listening to secular music; you're full of the devil; you've come to this church and tried to play — and that's why the whole service is off. It's no wonder when we get to the end of a service, you don't know what to play. You haven't been spiritually participating in the service."

About that time, they started getting aggravated. I added, "You'd better put that rebellion out of your heart and repent of it, because I can feel it — and I'm going to cast it out in front of this whole congregation if you don't get right with God!"

I rebuked them as if the title of my message were, "We're Going To Rebuke the Musicians." The point was, *they knew better!*

## Genuine Love Means Godly Rebuke

Someone said, "Pastor, that's hard." I know it's hard, but when God called me, He did not give me the option of running the church the way I want to run it. If we genuinely love people, we will rebuke them if we want to save them from spiritual destruction. Today I am glad to report those same musicians are flowing in a powerful anointing and are blessing thousands.

There are many people in God's house today who were once leaders but backslid and ran off. Why? When they continued in sin, no one rebuked them, so they persisted on toward the way of destruction.

A rebuke is not supposed to be *pleasant* to the natural emotions. Sometimes when you rebuke people, they will complain, "I don't like the way you said it!" I always reply, "That means I did it right. If you liked it, it wasn't a good rebuke."

## A Revelation About Rebuke

We find a revelation on rebuke in Titus 1:10,11:

**For there are many unruly and vain talkers and deceivers, specially they of the circumcision:**
**Whose mouths must be stopped, who subvert whole houses....**

Do you realize those are words that will set the captives free? Can you picture someone getting a good revelation on that scripture, walking into a church, going up to one of those "vain talkers and deceivers," and saying, "Shut your big mouth! The word of the Lord to you is, 'Get a grip on your lip! Don't talk to anyone!'"

During the first days of the Early Church, services were customarily held in homes; therefore, the reference to "whole houses." Verse 12 points out that entire churches have been destroyed by a few rebellious people:

**...teaching things which they ought not, for filthy lucre's sake.**

## New Testament Christianity Will Reappear

We're coming to the last days, and you had better get ready. Today's wimpy Christianity is going to disappear, to be replaced by the potent New Testament brand!

In the New Testament, we find where Paul went to Peter and boldly confronted him when Peter slipped into error about a few issues. Although Peter was one of the leading preachers of the day, Paul walked up to him in front of a crowd and wrote later, "I withstood him to his face." (See Galatians 2:11.)

Today, when some greedy preacher is in the middle of a meeting, manipulating everyone with his vain and deceitful words, a true man of God needs to walk in the door and say, "In the Name of God, you need to repent for the way you're dealing with these people!"

## Some Choice Advice From Paul

Paul's advice to Titus continues in verse 12:

**One of themselves, even a prophet of their own, said, The Cretians are always liars, evil beasts, slow bellies.**

Isn't that interesting? There are always prophets "of their own" in these rebellious groups. However, you are not a prophet unless you are under covering. Many people think that being under covering means "I *informed* someone that this is what I'm getting ready to do." No, being under a covering means you *ask* first. Otherwise, you're just your own prophet.

Verse 13 continues:

**This witness is true. Wherefore rebuke them sharply, that they may be strong in the faith.**

"Rebuke" means "to strike swiftly, verbally." Paul says that those who are in error and are teaching error should be confronted verbally — swiftly and sharply. That means the person is not going to like it when a rebuke comes.

Titus must have pastored a lot of people who needed to be rebuked, because in Titus 2:15, Paul advises:

**These things speak, and exhort, and rebuke with all authority. Let no man despise thee.**

## Authorized by God

Do you know why some churches are not prospering? Their ministers are not authorized to do what they're doing! They heard someone teach or preach some topic they liked, so they self-appointed and self-anointed themselves to do the same. Operating outside of God's flow, they take that truth and use it as their own, thinking that God will honor it because it is truth. However, just because you teach someone else's truth doesn't mean it is real to you or that God will automatically honor it. You must be *authorized* by God to carry that truth.

For example, you can go through Police Cadet School training and learn everything there is about being a policeman, learn how to shoot a gun, and learn all the laws of the land — but if you are not *authorized* to hold that office, you have only taken some training and acquired some information.

Paul advised Titus, "When you have the authority, rebuke with all authority and let no man despise you."

## Judas on the Road of No Return

Judas went down the road of no return, yet he was as close to Jesus as a person could get. Judas was handling all of Jesus' money. He was on the inside. He knew everything.

Furthermore, Jesus didn't call Judas while he was filled with the devil. Acts 1:17 quotes the other disciples as saying, "Judas had a portion with us. He was numbered with us. He had a ministry with us." In Matthew 10:4, Judas was listed among those who were anointed by Jesus to go and cast out devils. Surely Jesus didn't call someone full of the devil to go cast out the devil!

The Bible is very plain in John 13:27 that at the Last Supper, after Jesus and His disciples dipped into the cup and broke the bread, Satan entered the heart of Judas. At that point, Jesus turned and told Judas, "What you are getting ready to do, go and do quickly."

Just because you were close to the Lord at one time in your life does not mean you are still intimate with Him today. Judas was close to the Lord, and he didn't make it. Why? Judas, the keeper of the common purse, was upset because Jesus didn't spend the money the way *he* thought it should have been spent. As is always true with a person like that, he was the one who had the greedy heart, not Jesus. In fact,

Judas the "accountant" was stealing from the common purse, John says in John 12:6!

I have learned that when you develop an attitude against the covering God gives you, you allow it to cause a separation between you. Judas had a problem with Jesus.

Sometimes God's people need to be rebuked for their "poor" attitude. They sit in the church, talking about how God owns the cattle on a thousand hills, and stating, "Everything I need is *already* done." They say, "If you've got a problem, I know God will fix it for you."

But after the shouting dies down and the pastor announces it's time to receive the offering, they begin to murmur and complain.

Many Christians sit around and confess, "I'm the head and not the tail. I'm blessed coming in and blessed going out." And yet it often seems that we expect God to prosper us while we are still hoarding our money and allowing penny-pinching attitudes to rule when it comes to the things of God. Many say they are blessed, yet they never have anything to give. Their local church struggles to reach the lost or build a building because the members talk it but won't walk it.

## Poverty or Success?

The difference between our poverty mentality and the world's success mentality is very apparent in the way we train our young people. For example, I recently read about a "youth camp" the world held for their teenagers at a well-known hotel.

As you walked into the seminar, do you know what you saw? Rows and rows of computers! The kids were taught how to work the computers, how to market themselves, and how to invest in the stock market. I'm talking about 13- and 14-year-old kids!

Meanwhile, we've got our church kids swimming in a muddy pond someplace, and we call that a youth camp.

In addition to the substantial seminar fee, $100 extra was charged for the program on the last day. On that day, a chauffeured limousine picked up each young person and took him or her to a stock broker's firm, where they spent the day and actually placed an order. Afterwards, the chauffeured limousines took the young people back to the hotel for a nice dinner.

Those children were being indoctrinated to expect to be successful. Meanwhile, back at the church, if we try to get the parents of our teens to spend $5 on a book to go along with their lessons, some of the parents will complain.

They need to be rebuked for their poor attitude, because when all is said and done, those worldly trained kids will grow up and own the grocery stores, and the church kids will be praying that their check comes in on the third so they can buy some groceries there.

Many of God's people have developed a poverty mentality and need to be rebuked for it. If we're going to be blessed, let's be blessed!

## The Chastening of the Lord

**And ye have forgotten the exhortation which speaketh unto you as unto children, My son, despise not thou the chastening of the Lord, nor faint when thou art rebuked of him:**

**For whom the Lord loveth he chasteneth, and scourgeth [or whips] every son whom he receiveth.**

**If ye endure chastening, God dealeth with you as with sons; for what son is he whom the father chasteneth not?**

**But if ye be without chastisement [correction and rebuke], whereof all are partakers, then are ye bastards, and not sons.**

**Furthermore we have had fathers of our flesh which corrected us, and we gave them reverence: shall we not much rather be in subjection unto the Father of spirits, and live?**

**For they verily for a few days chastened us after their own pleasure; but he for our profit, that we might be partakers of his holiness.**

**Now no chastening for the present seemeth to be joyous, but grievous: nevertheless afterward it yieldeth the peaceable fruit of righteousness unto them which are exercised [or trained] thereby.**

**Hebrews 12:5–11**

Chastening is something you have to endure; you probably are not going to enjoy it. But if you do endure it, something comes "afterward."

## The Fruits of Discipline

You can tell when a child is properly disciplined. He may not always act perfectly, but you can still tell the difference between his behavior and that of a child who is left to run wild. You can also go into a church and tell whether the people are being properly trained or not.

**Wherefore lift up the hands which hang down, and the feeble knees;**
**And make straight paths for your feet, lest that which is lame be fumed out of the way [that is the road of no return]; but let it rather be healed....**
**Looking diligently lest any man fail of the grace of God; lest any root of bitterness springing up trouble you, and thereby many be defiled.**

**Hebrews 12:12,13,15**

People can become bitter very easily. Then they get into so much pride and need to be rebuked.

There are certain warning signs to look for in your life that indicate you are refusing correction. A person who refuses correction is what the Bible calls "a bastard child" — someone who is without correction; someone who is without a father.

## Warning Signs Against Error

The first thing that happens when you won't receive correction is that you attract *the spirit of error.* That's according to First John 4:6.

Many people in churches get off into error and say, "Well, I'm right; I'm right." They got into a spirit of error because they didn't have anyone around them who was able to correct them.

The second thing that happens when you won't receive correction is that you develop *bitterness.* Rebuke comes to produce a contrite, broken, submitted, and willing heart before God.

However, if you are not careful, you will allow the enemy to convince you that you shouldn't have had that rebuke; that no one should talk to you that way — who do these people think they are? And you will become bitter very quickly. You have to watch that.

The disorderly, the unorganized, and the irreverent despise instruction; especially when it comes in the form of correction. We have found, however, that godly people interested in a quality relationship with God appreciate the order and structure of the Holy Spirit.

The rebellious may respond to correction by stirring up discontent, resistance, or rebellion against authority — what the Bible terms "sedition."

## The Error of Sedition

When rebuked, the rebellious who are operating in sedition go to some of their friends and say, "Can you believe what So-and-so said to me? Can you believe what that usher did to me? Can you believe how Pastor Pitts preached?"

And some of them reply, "Yeah, yeah, yeah."

"Well, let's see if we can get ten friends together," the rebellious leader suggests — and the outcome is, all of them get into spiritual bondage together.

People are really something today. When you rebuke some, they talk back. Talking back is another sign a person won't receive rebuke. Rebuke is not a dialogue, but some people always have something to add, or they want to argue. They need to receive a rebuke and then go on. They need to allow God to correct them.

## Having Your Own Way

*Variance* is another manifestation of the rebellious. Variance causes strife. It is not overt but covert. Variance is a subtle form of rebellion. It means a person *varies* from what the Word of the Lord is for the house of God. Make no mistake, God has a word for the house.

I am not referring to how you run your own house; you should have had enough teaching to understand that a church is not supposed to control your personal affairs; but God has a word for His house.

When headship ministry communicates the vision, direction, and strategy of the Lord, the rebellious hearer is not convinced of it. Therefore he acts like he's following, but he's actually going to "vary" from these instructions slightly so he can do it *his own way.*

I was conducting a school of Bible classes once, and a person brought me three subjects he wanted to teach. I knew which subject he wanted to teach the most. I, being a good pastor, and he, being a new teacher, I wanted to make sure he could receive instruction and work under authority. So I chose the course I thought he should teach, although it wouldn't have been his first choice, to see how he would react.

A few weeks into the classes, I sat in to see what he was teaching. He was teaching the material *he* wanted to teach. He had simply put the name of the other course on it! He *varied.*

I took his class away from him *that* day. I said, "You're finished." Then I taught the class. We were quite blessed. *Variance.* It's rebellion.

An army can't operate that way, but churches try to function in the midst of variance and rebellion. If I tell someone, "I want you to sing two choruses before I preach," that means he or she should not vary and sing five choruses.

## Privates Don't Have All the Facts

Sometimes because we see where the ministry is going, we assume that gives us permission to proceed without permission, but it doesn't. What if an entire army troop was marching off somewhere and suddenly one of the privates said, "I see what we're going to do: We're going to march all the way around this hill. I'm going to step out of line, take a shortcut over the hill, and be the first one there."

He'll probably ruin the whole maneuver if he does. The enemy may be waiting in ambush for him on top of that hill! So you may think you see a situation correctly and be wrong. It is very probable you don't see the whole picture.

This individualistic attitude on the part of the congregation holds many churches back, because their leaders are spending too much time having to explain to everyone in *minute* detail what God is saying before they gain their cooperation.

Christians will never learn how to submit until a leader finally says, "This is what we're going to do, and that is what we're going to do, and you just need to get in line with it."

## Jealousy Toward Leaders

Did you know that some rebellion directs itself toward godly leaders? Some people actually want to "outdo" those over them. They are motivated by jealousy — a word that is sometimes translated as "emulation."

Emulation is when a person finds himself in ambitious competition with his headship. That's not a good spirit to have. You need to understand that *many people may have your gift, but no one has your calling.*

Have you ever been to an event that is supposed to be a gathering of many music ministries for the purpose of praising God, but it really turns into "the battle of the choirs" or "the battle of the pianist and the organist"? Each becomes progressively more carnal or louder, trying to outdo the other.

If you have a song to sing for the Lord, sing your song. The next person doesn't have to outdo you or sing better, faster, louder, or slower. He or she should just sing what God gives them to sing.

Some people actually become jealous of the authority, favor, or blessing of their pastor or other ministries of the Lord. They find themselves at odds, feeling insecure. Secretly they want the respect the church or this ministry possesses. What foolishness!

## The Unteachable

Some have an unteachable spirit. You can't tell them anything. You are considered unteachable when you reject or refuse to receive instruction. That's what Hebrews 12:25 says:

**See that ye refuse not him that speaketh. For if they escaped not who refused him that spake on earth, much more shall not we escape, if we turn away from him that speaketh from heaven.**

The last sign that you won't receive correction is when you despise the chastening and rebuke of the Lord. Naturally, chastening and rebuke are not pleasant experiences we seek out, but the Bible tells us that even though they are not pleasant, we should not despise them.

Correction and rebuke may hurt our feelings, and they may upset our emotions, but we learn valuable spiritual lessons through experiencing them.

We must not be so soft as to think anything that hurts our feelings is not of God. In your spirit you must learn to thank God that He cares enough about you to give you a pastor who will rebuke you at the appropriate times in the spirit of love — and that rebuke will yield *the peaceable fruit of righteousness* in your life.

## How To Face the Future With Confidence

Every day in every place, destinies are being determined. Some plans are thwarted and some purposes are perversed, while others ascend to new heights of fulfillment and accomplishment.

Even today you are in a battle for your future. On one hand is fulfillment; on the other, frustration. One holds success, peace of mind, and longevity. The other produces failure, confusion, and short-lived happiness. You hold the keys! You can choose. Others may *contribute* to your destiny, but you *determine* it!

Circumstances, people, money, and a variety of things may enhance or hinder your plan, but your decisions are the force that governs them. When you commit your plans to the Lord, you will succeed.

With the counsel you have received in this book, you will be able to pursue God's best and march toward tomorrow with confidence.

Knowing how to break the assignment of spiritual assassins is essential for those who will dare to pursue the ultimate — life in the flow of God.

**Through wisdom is an house builded; and by understanding it is established:**

**And by knowledge shall the chambers be filled with all precious and pleasant riches.**

**A wise man is strong; yea, a man of knowledge increaseth strength.**

**For by wise counsel thou shalt make thy war: and in multitude of counselors there is safety.**

**Proverbs 24:3–6**

## Other Books by Michael Pitts

*Don't Curse Your Crisis*

*Breaking Ungodly Soul Ties*

*Help! I Think God is Trying to Kill Me*

*A Dictionary of Contemporary Words and Concepts*

*Making the Holy Spirit Your Partner*

*Living on the Edge*

To purchase books, tape series, videos, and other
product materials by Michael Pitts please visit our
web site at www.cornerstonechurch.us